Scott Millard

Introduction
to Serials Work
for Library Technicians

D1051854

Pre-publication
REVIEWS,
COMMENTARIES,
EVALUATIONS . . .

"Scott Millard should be commended for synthesizing the complicated process of serials work into a readable and usable book. This book will be useful for anyone trying to understand how serials are acquired and processed in libraries. The use of modules is an interesting and effective organization of the material. The modules can be easily referenced in local training materials to produce a very helpful training manual for new employees. Many library training manuals concentrate only on the 'how to' of work without offering any understanding of the 'why.' This book covers both."

Karen Jander, MLIS
Senior Academic Librarian,
Serials Department,
Golda Meir Library,
University of Wisconsin at Milwaukee

"Scott Millard's informative book covers the life cycle of serials, from acquisitions and ordering to cataloging, claims, and renewals. This book is sure to provide practical help to the library technician who is involved in serials control on a regular or an occasional basis. The detailed glossary will be referred to often. The author has years of experience in conveying information regarding the technical aspects of library work. This text is a result of his work in this expanding field."

Dolores T. Harms Penner, MLS
Program Manager,
Library and Information
Technician Program,
Mohawk College of Applied Arts
and Technology,
Ontario, Canada

More pre-publication
REVIEWS, COMMENTARIES, EVALUATIONS . . .

"In his book, Scott Millard uses twelve
modules to clarify the process, procedures, and standards involved in serials work. Each module states a learning objective, then continues on to
cover such topics as acquisitions, ordering, receiving, cataloging, processing (shelving), claims, binding, renewals, cessations, automation, and new
technologies. The author introduces the
student to library tools such as *Ulrich's
International Periodicals Directory* and
AACR2. Sample forms are included for
small libraries using manual systems,
and there is also a glossary of terms. Librarians and support staff involved in
training library technical assistants will
find this book a useful tool."

Amber Hewette, MLIS
*Systems/Technical Services Librarian,
Southern Illinois University
School of Law Library*

The Haworth Information Press®
An Imprint of The Haworth Press
New York • London • Oxford

Introduction
to Serials Work
for Library Technicians

THE HAWORTH INFORMATION PRESS
Serials Librarianship
Jim Cole and Wayne Jones
Senior Editors

E-Serials: Publishers, Libraries, Users, and Standards, Second Edition by Wayne Jones

Journals of the Century edited by Tony Stankus

E-Serials Collection Managment: Transitions, Trends, and Technicalities by David C. Fowler

Introduction to Serials Work for Library Technicians by Scott Millard

Introduction
to Serials Work
for Library Technicians

Scott Millard

The Haworth Information Press®
An Imprint of The Haworth Press
New York • London • Oxford

Published by

The Haworth Information Press®, an imprint of The Haworth Press, Inc., 10 Alice Street, Binghamton, NY 13904-1580.

Cover design by Lora Wiggins.

Library of Congress Cataloging-in-Publication Data

Millard, Scott, 1958-
Introduction to serials work for library technicians / Scott Millard.
p. cm.
Includes bibliographical references and index.
ISBN 0-7890-2154-4 (alk. paper)—ISBN 0-7890-2155-2 (pbk : alk. paper)
1. Serials librarianship. 2. Serials control systems. 3. Libraries—Special collections—Serial publications. 4. Library technicians. I. Title.
Z692.S5M55 2004
025.3'432—dc22
                                                      2003021015

CONTENTS

Chapter 1. Introduction to Serials Work   **1**

What Is a Serial?   1
Common Characteristics of Serials   3
Problems with Serials   4

Chapter 2. Acquisitions   **15**

How to Find Out About Serials   15
Acquisition of a Serial   17
Finding Bibliographic Information for Serials   18
Verification   18

Chapter 3. Ordering   **25**

Information Needed for Ordering   25
Types of Orders   29

Chapter 4. Receipt and Check-In of Serials   **37**

Paper, CD-ROM, Microfiche, or Microfilm Format Serials   37
Principles of the Check-In System   39
Information Generally Found in a Check-in System   39
Recording Holdings Information   41

Chapter 5. Cataloging   **65**

Problems with the Full Cataloging of Serials   65
Alternatives to Cataloging   66
Cataloging Serials   74
Cataloging Internet Serials   88
Cataloging Standards   90

Chapter 6. Processing and Shelving Arrangements   **97**

Shelving Policies   99
Types of Shelving   102
How to Shelve   103

Chapter 7. Claims   105

Reasons for Placing Claims   105
Placing Claims   106
When to Claim   108

Chapter 8. Binding   111

Factors to Consider Before Binding   111
Preparing for Binding   113

Chapter 9. Renewals   117

Renewal Terminology   117
Handling Renewals   119

Chapter 10. Cessations   123

Title Changes   123
Cancellations   124

Chapter 11. Automation   127

Advantages of Automation   127
Disadvantages of Automation   128

Chapter 12. New Technology   131

Archiving   132
Storage   132
Equipment   132
Check-In   133
Access   133

Glossary   135

Bibliography   141

Index   145

ABOUT THE AUTHOR

Scott Millard, BA, MA, MLIS, is Manager of Library Services at Halton Catholic District School Board, Oakville, in Ontario, Canada. In his fifteen years of work with the Toronto Reference Library, he aided the conversion of a manual check-in system to an automated one. He continued to work with serials for several more years before concentrating on reference services. He also taught several courses in library and information sciences at Mohawk College in Hamilton, Ontario. He has taught introduction to libraries, introduction to reference work, multimedia resources, subject analysis, and serials.

Chapter 1

Introduction to Serials Work

Objective: Upon successful completion of this chapter, the student will have demonstrated the ability to identify serial publications and to describe the challenges of serials management in libraries.

Serials is one area of library work in which all the specialized training of a library and information technician graduate can be used to the fullest. Serials work requires a great deal of attention to detail. To be successful, you must be able to work accurately and quickly and have solid problem-solving abilities. You must also recognize that the effect of mistakes goes beyond the bounds of the serials department. The library customer usually finds the mistake and is inconvenienced.

The role that the library technician plays when dealing with serials varies from library to library. In a small library, the library technician may handle all aspects of serials work: ordering, cataloging, processing, claiming, renewing, problem solving. In other libraries, the technician may be assigned only one of these tasks. Other tasks, such as ordering, may be left to the librarian or other technicians. In some libraries, individual jobs are even more specific. A technician may be responsible only for checking serials in. No matter what role the technician plays, his or her contribution is important because serials work is an integral part of any library's operations.

WHAT IS A SERIAL?

To understand serials, we must first look at the definition of a serial. For this definition, we can consult the *Anglo-American Cataloguing Rules,* Second Edition, 2002 revision **(AACR2):**

Serial. A continuing resource issued in a succession of discrete parts, usually bearing numbering, that has no predetermined conclusion. Examples of serials include journals, magazines, electronic journals, continuing directories, annual reports, newspapers, and monographic series. (Appendix D-7)

We must examine several elements of this definition in detail:

- *A serial is a publication in any medium:* Serials used to come only in paper copies. Then came microfiche and microfilm. Now serials come in all of these formats and also in CD-ROM and online versions. A serial is not limited by format.
- *A serial is usually issued in successive parts:* A serial has many parts that are issued successively. For example, the January 1995 issue is published first, followed by the February 1995 issue, which is followed by the March 1995 issue, etc.
- *These successive parts usually bear numeric or chronological designations:* Somewhere on the serial there will (should) be a designation that gives you some idea as to how this issue fits into the serial as a whole. This designation could be a date, as is used with newspapers (e.g., February 16, 1995). The designation could simply be a month and year (e.g., February 1995). In many cases, the designation also involves volumes and numbers (e.g., volume 4 number 1). A **chronological designation** often accompanies volumes and numbers such as vol. 4 no. 1 1995. (You will also see this written as vol. 4, no. 1, 1995.) Sometimes, no designation is found on a particular issue. The publisher may simply have forgotten to include this information.
- *A serial is intended to be continued indefinitely:* If the publisher has determined that there will be an end to the particular publication—the publication will cease after a certain number of issues—then it is not a serial. Historical dictionaries or encyclopedias that are published over many years but that have a predetermined ending are not serials. An example of this type of publication is the *Dictionary of the Middle Ages* (New York: Scribner, 1982-1989), which was to be published in thirteen volumes only.
- *Serials include periodicals, newspapers, annual publications, publications of societies, and monograph series.* We generally associate serials with **periodicals** and **annuals.** Serials, how-

ever, include newspapers and other publications of societies, such as their reports, lists of members, etc. Serials may also include monograph series. A **monograph series** is a "group of separate items related to one another by the fact that each item bears, in addition to its own title proper, a collective title applying to the group as a whole" (AACR2, Appendix D-7). An example of this is the *Historical Dictionary of Mozambique* (Metuchen, NJ: Scarecrow Press, 1991). This is a monograph. However, it is also volume 47 of the series *African Historical Dictionaries.*

Therefore, when working with serials, you can handle a wide variety of material including periodicals, timetables, **proceedings,** and others. For customers, and often for library employees, serials terminology can be very confusing. We use the terms serial, journal, periodical, proceeding, newsletter, brief, and magazine, among others, to refer to various types of serials. Library technicians may see a difference among these terms, but the general public does not. For the purposes of this book, we will use the general term "serial" unless we are referring to a particular type of serial. For definitions of serials terminology, please consult the glossary.

COMMON CHARACTERISTICS OF SERIALS

Several characteristics are common to all serials regardless of what they are called or how often they are published.

1. *Serials are issued in successive parts:* This means that each serial requires a continuous routine of receiving, tracking through some sort of check-in process, renewing, processing, and shelving.
2. *Completeness is important to the overall usefulness of serials:* Eventually, we tend to discard titles with a poor receipt record because a serial with missing issues is not very useful to our customers.
3. *The cost of serials is greater than the cost of monographs:* Costs are higher for serials than for monographs because serials represent a continuous commitment of time, space, and money. Some

journals cost as much as $6,000 to $8,000 a year per subscription. Some only cost $20, but each requires much more handling, shelf space, and staff time than a monograph. This increases the financial commitment an institution must make each time it places a journal subscription.

4. *Serials have poor bibliographic control:* Generally, you can find a book you want to order listed in *Books in Print* or a related resource unless you are in a very specialized field. For serials, on the other hand, *no single place to get all the bibliographic information exists.* Even having an issue on hand does not guarantee that you have all the information needed to order the serial or that the information provided in the issue is complete and accurate. The publisher may have moved, the serial may have ceased publication, etc. A great deal of detective work is often necessary to locate missing information.

5. *Serial titles may present several problems:* Titles may be non-descriptive, such as *Bulletin* or *Newsletter,* or consist of an acronym or initialism, such as *RUSI Journal.* In some cases, the same title may be given to two or more serials that are not related. For example, there is a *London Magazine* published in London, Ontario, as well as one published in London, England. When you place an order, you must make sure that you are actually ordering the serial you want. Although you can often rely on unique numbers assigned to each distinct title (the ISSN— **International Standard Serial Number**) to identify a specific title, the assignment of these numbers is abused or ignored in some cases. This adds to the difficulties in identifying like titles.

PROBLEMS WITH SERIALS

Serials work tends to be much more problematic than monographs work. Many of the problems encountered when working with serials relate to the nature of serial publications. What can happen to a serial throughout its lifetime that causes problems for libraries?

A Serial May Never Be Published

To understand this problem, we must first examine how a serial originates. Someone originates the idea for a new serial. He or she sends an announcement to professors, librarians, or anyone who expresses an interest in this new title. This generally happens a year or so before the first issue is to appear. There is also a call for papers—a request for articles from people who would like to have their material published in the new serial. Depending upon the interest shown in the serial through requests for sample issues or for subscriptions, the decision is made whether to publish the serial. If there is a decided lack of interest, the publisher, who most often is interested in making a profit, may decide not to proceed.

Various other problems can lead to the serials never being published. The editors or even the publisher may experience a financial setback. It usually takes three to four years for a successful research journal to begin to break even. The first years are costly to the company, and many publishers do not survive.

Some serials are edited or published by societies or associations that do not do the actual printing of the serial. Instead, the society contacts a commercial publisher to print the journal. In the case of a new serial, perhaps the society and the publisher of choice are unable to reach an agreement. A lengthy delay sometimes occurs while the society searches for another publisher.

For a wide variety of reasons, the serial may never be published. Unfortunately, those who have placed orders or who have expressed interest in the serial are usually not notified of this change in plan. In the library, we wait (and wait and wait) for the first issue to arrive. Perhaps, many months later, we learn that the serial is not to be published.

Title Changes

Some serials appear to have as many titles as they do issues. There are several reasons for these title changes:

1. The serial may get a new editor. This means that the focus of the serial may change, and the title may change to express this new focus.
2. A new cover design often brings about a change in the name of the serial. The editors feel compelled to change the name to reflect the new look. In most cases, the serial itself does not change;

the serial continues to reflect the same policies and views. Only the cover and title have changed.

3. Many serials are published by government bodies, and the names of government bodies often change. For example, a government may amalgamate two or more departments. With this change in the publishing body, the outlook of the serial may change, which will lead to a new title. Also, since so many of these items are simply titled *Report of the* (name of the government body), the change in the name of the government body changes the title.

4. The scope of the journal may change, for example, from national to international or vice versa. To reflect this new scope, the title may also change.

5. In some cases, once the publisher has established the title of a journal, he or she may discover that it resembles too closely the title of another journal. To avoid confusion, he or she may change the title. Hopefully, the publisher will inform you of this change in advance.

Serials May Merge Permanently or Temporarily

Titles merge for a variety of reasons:

* societies with similar interests may join to publish a title;
* a publisher of two titles in one field of interest may find the resources to continue only one title;
* publishers may merge;
* a serial may be absorbed by a competitor.

In all of these cases, the library will need to exert some sort of control over the serials that have merged. A word of warning: just because you have a subscription to one of these serials does not mean that you will continue to receive the new serial.

You must check with your supplier to ensure that the library will continue to receive the new serial if it is wanted. In rare cases, two serials may merge for one issue only. Recording this information is a problem.

The Serial May Split into Two or More Separate Serials

In some cases, the field covered by the serial becomes too large or new fields emerge with their own publication possibilities. This is quite common in science and medicine. For example, *Jane's Weapon Systems* split into *Jane's C 3 I Systems* and *Jane's Underwater Warfare Systems* since demand merited separate, specialized serials. Trying to cover all weapons systems in a single serial proved to be impossible.

Societies that publish a common serial may have a "falling out" with each other. As a result, the serial that they publish jointly splits. Each society now publishes its own serial.

The Serial May Be Suspended

Publishers may suspend a serial, meaning that the publication has been temporarily placed on hold. This suspension could last for a few months to several years. The publisher intends to revive the suspended serial. There are many reasons for a **suspension:**

1. The publisher (usually a small press or society) may run out of money. While the publisher attempts to get money from other sources, the serial is not published.
2. The physical plant undergoes changes or upgrades. For the duration of this upgrading, the machines are not functioning and the serial is suspended.
3. The editor resigns or dies, and no obvious or immediate replacement is forthcoming. This is a concern for small presses where, in most cases, the editor produces the serial himself or herself.

The Serial May Cease Publication

In contrast to a suspended serial, which the publisher still intends to publish, the serial that has ceased publication is, in effect, dead. The publisher does not plan to continue producing it. This is one of the most common problems with serials, and one of the most difficult to resolve. In many cases, no notification from the publisher informs subscribers that a serial has ceased. We learn that the serial has ceased when we submit a claim for a missing issue. In some cases, despite repeated attempts to locate the publisher, we are unable to inquire about the fate of the publication. The following are some of the most common reasons for **cessations:**

1. The publisher may run out of money and can no longer publish the serial.
2. The publisher may lose interest in the serial and cease publishing it. This is especially common with small, one-person publishers.
3. The publisher may fail to keep pace with the ever-changing field covered by the serial. Publishers in fields where currency is crucial, such as medicine or science, may encounter this problem. For a serial to survive, there must be a demand for it, meaning someone must be willing to pay for a subscription. If the publisher does not keep up with current trends in the field, the serial is no longer useful. Subscribers cancel subscriptions and the publisher faces financial loss. In some fields, such as medicine, even the loss of a few subscribers can force the cessation of a serial.
4. Sometimes, especially when dealing with small publishing houses, the publisher may simply disappear. Suddenly your serial is no longer being received. When you try to claim the missing issues, your claims are returned. The publisher has left no forwarding address. Unfortunately, you do not know whether the publisher has simply moved and the serial will continue, or whether the publisher has gone out of business. Unless the library staff decides how to handle such cases, many hours can be wasted trying to locate publishers.

Usually, cessations are extremely difficult to confirm. Frequently, the publisher will not announce the journal's demise. You may write to the publisher, perhaps more than once, before the cessation is confirmed. Subscription **agents,** companies that look after a library's serial subscriptions and act as liasons between library and publisher, can help in finding out what has ceased.

The Format of the Serial May Change

With the increasing availability of microfilm, microfiche, and CD-ROM, the format in which the serial is published can change throughout its run. The most common format change is in the size of the serial. The serial may go from a regular size serial to a **folio** (any size that will not fit on normal shelving). This poses a problem for shelving. Do you shelve the whole run of the serial in the folio section (the area established by the library to house items that cannot be accommodated in the regular stacks), or do you put only the new issues in the folio section? If you choose the latter, you must provide sufficient signage to direct the customer from one section to the other.

Recently, some serials have changed from print to CD-ROM or other electronic formats. This causes problems not only for shelving and signage (directing customers from one format to the other) but also for cataloging. In theory, each format requires a separate catalog record. The records need to be linked so that customers and staff know what is available in which format. You may require additional computer equipment to access the new formats.

Formats May Be Different for Different Years

Libraries may receive a serial in several different formats. For example, the library staff may decide to get the current year in paper copy, which facilitates browsing, while other issues are only found in microfilm to permit easy storage of the material. If you have ever tried to browse a magazine on microfiche, you know why the paper format is preferable for this purpose.

In some libraries, as we try to build the collection by purchasing back issues (issues that are not current), we realize that we may need to buy several different formats. The easiest way to acquire back issues is through dealers who offer these issues on film or fiche. To further complicate matters, some vendors offer certain issues of the same serial on film while other issues are on microfiche. When dealing with film, you may need to order both 35mm and 16mm to acquire a complete set. All of these formats require different storage facilities and different readers (the equipment needed to use the microfilm or fiche). You may also need individual catalog records for each format with linking notes depending upon library cataloging policies.

In some cases, although the serial itself does not change format, a **supplement** to an issue may be in fiche, film, or CD-ROM format. This raises several problems: how to record this information in either the **kardex** (a serial check-in system) or the catalog; how to link the serial to the supplement; how to inform the customer of this aberration; and where to physically put the fiche, film, or CD-ROM. Some library staffs conclude that these supplements are simply too time consuming and bothersome and therefore decided that the easiest means of handling them is simply to discard them.

The Frequency of the Serial May Change

When we first acquire a serial, we note the **periodical frequency** of publication: quarterly, biannually, annually, etc. We also note when the issues are generally published: every April, in January and June, monthly, etc. This publication pattern allows us to predict when the next issue of a certain serial should be arriving. However, for many reasons, the publication dates or the frequency pattern may change.

We expect to receive a serial at certain times of the year. Suddenly, we receive an issue of the serial at a different time. The publisher, for any number of reasons, may decide to change the publication pattern. This seemingly minor change requires extensive adjustments to our serial records.

The publisher may also change the frequency of publication. A former quarterly may become an annual. Or the annual serial, due to high demand, may become a quarterly. This also requires us to change our serial records. Unfortunately, changes in frequency happen often. To further complicate the matter, the publication frequency can change more than once. For example, the publisher of an annual serial may have more articles to publish than the serial can accommodate, so he or she decides to publish quarterly. However, two years later a shortage of material occurs, so a switch to biannual frequency is made. Two years later, it is back to annual. Each change requires extensive housekeeping of serial records.

The Serial May Have Supplements

Supplements—additional material that accompanies a particular issue of a serial—often cause more problems than they are worth.

Some library personnel take the easy way out when dealing with supplements: they simply discard them.

The biggest problem with supplements is their infrequency. Supplements are generally irregular and difficult to track. This problem is augmented in many cases because no presence of a supplement is indicated in the issue that the supplement accompanies. For example, a supplement comes with the April issue. However, in the April issue, no mention of the supplement exists. If for some reason you failed to receive the supplement, you would not know it since there is no record of the supplement's existence. You can, therefore, never be sure if a supplement accompanies an issue or not. Claiming a supplement is always confusing.

Recording the supplement is also a problem. On a kardex we can usually record the existence of the supplement. In an automated system, we need to either create a separate record for the supplement or record the supplement's existence in a note. Either method is time consuming and not wholly satisfactory. Creating a record for an item that may never come in again is a waste of time. Adding a note to the record is problematic because, in most cases, notes are added at the end of the main record that lists all of the holdings (i.e., the actual volumes held by the library). Therefore, the supplement's record will always be at the end of the main record with no link between the supplement and the issue it accompanied.

Other problems are associated with supplements:

- A single issue may have more than one supplement.
- A supplement may have a distinctive title, in which case you may want to catalog the supplement as a monograph. Some link will still be necessary between the monograph and the serial issue it accompanied.
- In some cases, simply identifying a supplement is a problem. With many serials, especially travel magazines, advertisements accompany the issues. Often these advertisements are quite elaborate. They appear to be supplements. Deciding which is a supplement and which is an advertisement can be difficult.

In short, supplements are a challenge for record keeping, claiming, and cataloging.

The Serial May Have Indexes

One special type of supplement is the index. Indexes are often published as annual supplements to the serial and are separate publications that come with the serial. However, all indexes are not this straightforward. Many serials have the index in an actual issue of the serial. A serial may publish the annual index for the past year in the April issue of the next year (e.g., the 1994 index is in the April 1995 issue), or the publisher may publish a new index every few years. Other serials have no indexes at all.

Indexes create several problems:

- The index may not be included with the subscription to the serial. You may have to order the index separately. This means that you must wait for the announcement of the publication of the index and then order it. You must also factor in any additional costs in the library budget.
- The index may be included in an issue in the following year. For example, the 1994 index may be included in the April 1995 issue. How should you record this information?
- The index may be published irregularly. This requires that you check the serial on a regular basis to see if an announcement of the publication of the index can be found.
- Indexes often create binding nightmares. When you have a complete set of a serial, you usually want to bind it immediately before any issues are lost. However, if the index is not published until the following April, you have a choice. You can bind the serial in December, guaranteeing that you have a complete set and then bind the index separately. Or you can wait until April of the following year and bind the index with the issues but risk losing an issue of the serial in the meantime.

Serials May Change Their Enumeration

In most cases, volume 2 follows volume 1; issue number 4 follows issue number 3. However, in some cases the **enumeration** of the serial changes. Suddenly, volume 1 follows volume 28 or issue number 1 follows issue 6. The enumeration may change completely: last year's issues were vol. 4 no. 1, vol. 4 no. 2, etc., and this year's are

January 1995, March 1995, etc. A change in enumeration usually results when the publisher has made other changes in the serial, such as adding sections, changing the title, changing format or cover, or adding special supplements or issues.

Enumeration changes cause problems for library staff and the customer. The customer cannot understand why volume 1 follows volume 6, or why there are now two volumes designated as volume 1. The customer is unsure which volume 1 he or she wants. The staff's problem is how to record this information. The usual rule is to record the enumeration as it appears on the serial. You simply copy the information directly from the serial itself. However, to avoid any further confusion, a note is included in the record to explain the change in enumeration (e.g., beginning with 1995, volume 1 starts again).

The Serial May Come in Different Editions

Some serials come in different editions. For example, there is both a Canadian and an American edition of *Time*. Serials may also have Braille editions, regional editions (e.g., an Eastern edition), or international editions. For the serials unit, these different editions can cause problems. First, you have to ensure that you are actually ordering the edition that you want. In many cases, the orders will go to different addresses. Each edition should have a different ISSN (a unique number to identify a serial) and may have a different subscription address. However, the problems do not end with the ordering. We must carefully check each issue that arrives in the library to ensure that we *are* receiving the correct edition.

Some Serials, Especially Proceedings of an International Congress, Are Published As Monographs

An international congress is a gathering of experts in a particular field. The purpose of a congress is to facilitate the exchange of information and ideas, usually through the presentation of papers. These papers are then collected and published as the proceedings of the congress. Congresses are usually held annually. Many libraries collect these published papers since they offer the most current trends or thoughts in a particular field. However, quite often this collection of papers is also published as a monograph with a distinct title that is quite different from the title given to the serial publication. The customer and even the staff often know the proceedings only by this title. This presents a cataloging problem: how to record the special title so that we can access this item and, at the same time, note that it is part of a serial. There are no easy answers.

This confusion can also lead to the library's acquiring two copies of the same publication. The person responsible for collection development may order the monograph not knowing that it is also a serial that the library already receives. Alternatively, the library's subscription to the serial may not include the proceedings if they are published only as a monograph (and not as part of the serial). The library could miss a very important work simply because there is no clear indication of what is included in the subscription. A good rapport with the agent or the publisher is needed to avoid such lapses.

The Serial May Contain Parts of Another Serial or Monograph That Must Be Removed

Publishers want to send their information to us in the most efficient manner. Since they are already sending us a serial, they might as well save further postage and include a monograph or even another serial as part of the serial that we receive.

The Price of the Serial May Increase

The literature is full of articles on the soaring cost of journals. This is a problem most libraries have faced through the late 1970s and into the 1980s and 1990s. The problem is not confined to any one type of journal. In some subject areas such as science or medicine (where practitioners rely heavily on journals for their information), the problem is more acute and the price increases from one year to the next can be quite dramatic. These increases have come at the same time as budgets of most libraries are being drastically cut. Every April, *Library Journal* publishes a journal price index, which analyzes the price increases by category and subject. This can offer some help in trying to determine the possible price increases for the following year.

Chapter 2

Acquisitions

Objective: Upon successful completion of this chapter, the student will have demonstrated the ability to describe how to find out about serials and to verify serials for acquisitions.

HOW TO FIND OUT ABOUT SERIALS

One of the biggest problems we encounter when working with serials is discovering what serials are available to order. There is no single place to look to find a description of all the serials currently published. A serial of potential value to the library can be published for several years before anyone working at the library learns that the serial exists. When trying to track down serials of interest to library patrons, we must search a wide variety of sources. The following are some of the ways that we learn about serials.

1. *Sample Copies:* Publishers try their hardest to make library personnel aware of new serials. The publishers want to sell their products and get as many subscriptions as possible to defray the cost of publishing and to make a profit. One of the best ways to notify library staff of a new serial is to send a sample copy. Most often, sample copies arrive unsolicited, but sometimes they are requested. Usually no accompanying letter indicates that it is a sample copy, and staff time can be wasted in trying to process the copy. Eventually, we discover that it is a sample copy, and it should be routed to the appropriate person(s) for consideration. We always include a note indicating that it is a sample copy so that no further staff time is wasted.

Sample copies are the preferred means by which we evaluate a serial for possible acquisition. With the sample issue in hand, staff can examine all aspects of the serial: content, size, format, editorial point of view, cost, etc. The sample copy usually, but not always, includes all the information needed to acquire (place an order for) the serial.

2. *Flyers:* Publishers often distribute flyers announcing a new serial. This is the preferred way to advertise new serials when issues have not yet been published. The flyer gives the title, publisher, and cost, and often includes the frequency of publication. Unfortunately, the ISSN is not usually included since it may not yet have been assigned. A brief indication of the serial's content is noted, and any outstanding features, e.g., the serial is lavishly illustrated or the only serial in a new field, are highlighted.

Sometimes the flyer will allow you to reserve a sample copy when the first issue is published. If the library management decides to request a sample issue, we record this information somewhere so that once the sample arrives it can be quickly and easily identified as such. It is best to have all samples directed to one individual to lessen the possibility of confusion.

3. *Other Serials:* Instead of distributing a flyer, a publisher often places an advertisement announcing the new serial in an established journal that covers the same or a related field. The belief is that people who read the established serial may be interested in the new journal and will either subscribe or request a sample.

4. *Recommendations:* We should never forget the importance of recommendations from the public, staff members, or colleagues in other libraries. Libraries encourage this input from the public and colleagues by providing forms on which individuals can record recommended titles. Such recommendations should be considered very seriously.

5. *Selection materials:* Most of the materials used in book selection, such as *British Book News* or *Choice,* include reviews of new serials. These provide an excellent means of evaluating a serial without having the issue on hand. Having read a review, library staff will often request a sample from the publisher to conduct their own evaluations.

6. *Bibliographies:* Bibliographies pertaining to a specific field are often a good source of learning about serials in that subject area. Most often, for serials located in this way, a sample copy is requested for further evaluation.

7. *Newslists:* With the advent of newslists, library staff members can be informed of new serials quite quickly and simply. No longer are you limited to interaction with the staff in your physical library; you can be in touch through the Internet with library employees and publishers located anywhere in the world. Newslist members tend to share a common interest. Therefore, a newslist service can be used quite effectively to notify many people of the presence of a serial.

These are a few of the common methods we use to identify serials of potential interest to library patrons. You may also be browsing in a store and come across an interesting serial, or you may see an advertisement for a new serial on a bus or at a bus stop. In most cases, a sample copy should be requested so that you can evaluate the serial yourself.

ACQUISITION OF A SERIAL

The decision to acquire a serial is made after careful consideration. Purchasing, cataloging, and processing a monograph are all one-time costs. A serial, however, requires an ongoing commitment. A good serial collection should have a complete run of a serial if that title is to be useful. The impact of this principle on the budget is considerable. You pay not only for the initial subscription to a serial, but you continue to pay for that serial year after year. On top of this cost, we must consider the cost of cataloging the serial and its possible title changes, processing (an ongoing concern since each issue must be processed), binding (another ongoing concern), and all the staff time involved in claiming, paying invoices, etc. We must also take into account that the cost of serials continues to increase at an alarming rate. A serial that may have started out at $25 per year can quickly become a $50 per year serial. For journals offered in formats other than paper, we must have the appropriate equipment to access them. Therefore, the decision to subscribe to a serial must be made very carefully.

In most cases, two main reasons justify acquiring a new serial:

1. *Public demand:* If enough members of the public request a certain serial, the library should seriously consider acquiring that title. Obviously, a demand for it exists.

2. *Collection policy:* The **collection policy** is a written statement that outlines what the library will acquire. For example, if the collection policy states that the library is to acquire all regional travel material, any new regional travel serials should be acquired.

Often the collection policy will identify any restrictions placed on serials acquisitions. For example, the policy may state that any serial over $50 per year should be considered only if it satisfies further criteria, which would be clearly stated in the policy.

FINDING BIBLIOGRAPHIC INFORMATION FOR SERIALS

As with a book, basic bibliographic information about the serial must be ascertained before an order can be placed. For a serial, we require the following information: (1) current title and (2) publisher. The following information is also highly recommended:

- cost,
- frequency,
- ISSN, and
- any background information such as previous titles.

All of this information should be verified before placing an order. Doing so will help the supplier locate the specific serial that you wish to order. It will also avoid confusion among serials with like titles.

VERIFICATION

Verifying a title or searching for all the information mentioned previously is often the most difficult part of acquiring a serial. When verifying the title, the following points should be considered:

- Make sure that you have an accurate and complete title. Often the source that helped you to identify this serial will not provide you with full information about the title.

- Verify the availability of the title. Is it still in print? The serial may have already ceased publication.
- Determine if the serial is indexed and, if so, where. The usefulness of serials is dependent upon the ease with which their contents can be accessed. For most serials, the main means of providing access is through a periodical index either in print or online. If the library subscribes to a periodical index that indexes the serial, access to the serial's contents is assured. In other words, the serial will be used. If the serial is not indexed or if the library does not have an index that covers the serial's content, access is more difficult. Customers must go through many issues of the serial to locate articles of interest. The usefulness of the serial is questionable since most customers will not do this laborious searching. You should think twice about acquiring any serial that will be of limited use to your customers.
- Determine what formats are available: film, fiche, paper, or online and which format serves your customers' needs best.

The following sections discuss several helpful tools to check for the bibliographic information you need to order a title.

Ulrich's International Periodicals Directory

Ulrich's is an annual publication listing serials in print. It covers all countries and most types of serials. It includes annuals and controlled circulation serials (serials only available to a particular profession or limited to a geographic area). *Ulrich's* is available in paper, online, microfiche, and CD-ROM formats.

The serials in *Ulrich's* are arranged under subject headings such as *Interior design and decoration* or *Pharmacy and pharmacology* (although the information may change depending on edition consulted). In some cases, *Ulrich's* provides subheadings such as *Interior design and decoration-abstracting, bibliographies, statistics* and *Interior design and decoration-furniture and house furnishings* or *Medical science-dentistry* and *Medical science-endocrinology, etc.* Under each subject heading, the serials are listed alphabetically by title. If a serial is listed under more than one subject heading, it is described fully only once and cross-references are provided in other cases to refer you to the full description.

Ulrich's provides many aids to help the user locate serials of interest:

- Title index—Since *Ulrich's* is arranged by subject, if you know only the title, you need to consult the title index first to locate the page where the entry will be found.
- Cessation list—This is a list of serials that are no longer published. This list is useful in determining which serials have actually ceased.
- List of serials available on CD-ROM or online—This list helps you to determine which serials are available in what formats.
- List of subject headings used—This list helps you determine the subject heading used in *Ulrich's* for the topic in which you are interested. A cross-reference index alerts you to related topics that you may also wish to consult.
- ISSN index—If you have only the ISSN, you can identify the title through this index.
- Refereed serials—This list provides the names of serials for which articles are refereed or reviewed by peers. This guarantees that a certain quality of articles is maintained.

Ulrich's provides an extensive amount of information about each serial listed. All the information needed to order a serial can be found, including current title, previous titles (if any), publisher's name and address, formats available, frequency, year the publication began, list of indexes that index the serial, etc.

The introduction to *Ulrich's* is excellent. You should read this introduction, especially the information on interpreting entries.

The Serials Directory

The Serials Directory is an annual publication listing serials in print. It is comparable to *Ulrich's*. Serials in *The Serials Directory* are arranged under broad subject headings such as *Agriculture* (the information may change depending on the edition consulted). Often the broad subject categories are further divided, such as *Agriculture-abstracting, bibliographies and statistics; Agriculture-agricultural equipment; Agriculture-crop production and soil*, etc. This type of subject arrangement allows you to identify serials that are relevant to a particular topic. "See notes" refer you to relevant serials in another subject category. Within the subject categories, the entries are arranged in alphabetical order by the title of the serial.

The Serials Directory has extensive indexes to help the user:

- Newspaper listing—Newspapers are listed separately in *The Serials Directory*. They are first divided into American and non-American newspapers. The entries are then arranged by geographical location, and then alphabetically by title.
- Alphabetical title index—Since *The Serials Directory* is arranged by subject, this index allows you to identify the page on which the entry will be found if you know the title of a serial.
- ISSN index—If you have only the ISSN, you can use this index to identify the title of the serial.
- Peer-reviewed index—This index identifies the serials that are peer reviewed. In **peer-reviewed serials** each article submitted is reviewed by people who are considered to be experts in the appropriate field before being accepted for publication. For instance, a history professor might act as a reviewer for a history serial. The theory is that peer-reviewed serials are somewhat more scholarly since only those articles that meet the criteria of the reviewers and of the editorial board are included.
- Serials available on CD-ROM index—This is a handy index for libraries that are converting their collections to CD-ROM. This index allows you to identify the serials that are available on CD-ROM.
- Serials available online index—This allows you to identify serials that are available online through such dealers as DIALOG.
- Book review index—This identifies serials that include book reviews.
- Advertising-accepted index—Only certain serials accept advertising, and this index identifies them. This is important for businesspeople or publishers who wish to advertise their products.
- Controlled circulation index—Some serials are available only through a membership or are limited to a certain geographical location. These are called controlled circulation serials. It is important to be able to identify which serials are controlled circulation so that one does not waste time in trying to acquire titles that are not generally available.

- Copyright clearance center index—Some serials have registered with the Copyright Clearance Center (in the United States), which, in effect, handles the copyright for these serials.
- New title index—This index identifies new titles that have appeared since the last issue of the directory. This is useful for identifying new serials that the library may want to consider for acquisition.

The Serials Directory provides an extensive amount of information on each serial listed and is one of the best sources to consult for data on serials.

Standard Periodical Directory

The *Standard Periodical Directory* is a publication that includes American and Canadian serials. General newspapers are not covered in this source, but specialized newspapers, newsletters, directories, government publications, and consumer and trade publications are included.

In the *Standard Periodical Directory* periodicals are classified by subject (the information may change depending on the edition consulted). Within each subject listing, the titles of the periodicals are listed alphabetically. A list of the subject headings used is given at the front of each volume. A cross-index from subject headings not used to those actually used is provided. These help you to identify periodicals on a particular topic, which is useful for collection development. There is also a title index to allow you to identify quickly the whereabouts of the citation to a particular title. Within each entry, the information given is similar to that included in other serial directories. Before using the *Standard Periodical Directory,* you should read the introduction because it explains how to interpret the individual entries.

Gale Directory of Publications and Broadcast Media

The *Gale Directory of Publications and Broadcast Media* is an annual list of Canadian and American periodicals and newspapers (the information may change depending on the edition consulted). It excludes newsletters and directories. This resource is arranged by geographical location, first by country, then by state or province, and finally by city (e.g., Canada—Ontario—North Bay). Within each geographical location, the entries are arranged in alphabetical order by title.

This is an excellent source to consult for daily, weekly, and semi-weekly newspapers, daily periodicals, general magazines, foreign language periodicals, trade journals, technical publications, professional journals, fraternal newsletters, and specialized periodicals. Since it is arranged by geographical location, it is easy to determine which periodicals are published in any given locality. Several indexes facilitate use of this resource: subject indexes, a name and keyword index, and geographical references. Each entry contains the following information:

- a number assigned by the directory staff that is used in the indexes to identify a specific title
- title and subtitle (if appropriate)
- former titles (if appropriate)
- publisher's name, address, telephone, and fax number
- description of the coverage of the periodical
- date of first issue
- frequency
- printing method and other technical data
- names of key personnel such as editors
- ISSN
- advertising rates
- subscription information
- circulation data

It is highly recommended that you read the introduction to the *Gale Directory*.

These serial directories are the main resources in which to find the information necessary to order any serial. Many serials will not, however, be found in any of these directories. Several other resources are available that you may need to consult.

1. *Library catalogs:* Most libraries now make their catalogs available online. These can be accessed from other libraries through the Internet or other electronic networks. In many cases, the au-

tomated catalog includes serials. You can search these catalogs and, if you are lucky, find a library that owns and has cataloged the serial in question, thus accessing the basic information such as title, previous title, publisher, frequency, ISSN, and publication history (e.g., when did it start publication). The cost of the serial is usually not included in the cataloge record, but at least you now know to whom to direct further questions.

One great advantage of automated catalogs is that they are updated on a regular basis. Therefore, you can usually find current information on a serial by checking one or more sources. If you are looking for a technical serial, you will be more successful checking the catalog of a specialized library, e.g., the *National Library of Medicine* catalog is a likely source for a medical title. One disadvantage is that you are relying on cataloging information created by another institution. You may not be familiar with that library's standards of cataloging and must accept that the record may contain errors.

2. *Automated utilities:* Vendors of catalog records, such as OCLC (the Online Computer Library Center), make their databases of catalog records available online for a fee. These are excellent resources to consult. Many libraries already use one of these automated utilities for cataloging other library materials. However, this option is not practical for a small library not already using the services of a bibliographic utility.

3. *Other serials:* Some publications, themselves serials, are intended to help us gain some bibliographic control over the multitude of items being published by listing bibliographic information about items in a particular field of endeavor or published in a particular geographic area. Examples include *Canadiana, British National Bibliography,* and *British Archaeological Bibliography.* This type of serial may list serials, monographs, and other formats on a specific topic such as archaeology, or items published within a certain geographical area such as Great Britain. They try to be as comprehensive as possible. The price of publication is not usually given but publisher information is, providing you with a source to contact for further information about a particular serial.

Chapter 3

Ordering

Objective: Upon successful completion of this chapter, the student will have demonstrated the ability to order serials publications.

The library staff has decided to acquire a particular serial. You have verified the serial; that is, you have found all the information necessary to place the order. Orders must contain the information in the following section to ensure that the vendor and the library employee are discussing the same serial. Many serials have the same generic titles such as *Newsletter* or *Journal,* so it is especially important to supply the information described or as much of it as you have been able to ascertain.

INFORMATION NEEDED FOR ORDERING

Correct Title

If you are starting a subscription to a current title, make sure that you have the correct title. For a serial still in print, ensure that you have the current title and not an older one. If you record the wrong title, you may actually receive copies of the older title. At the very least, you will be in for a round of phone calls to the vendor trying to clarify the order. Likewise, if you are placing a back order and you want issues of a previous title, make sure that you record the exact title that you want.

ISSN (International Standard Serial Number)

The ISSN is a unique number assigned to each new serial title. Its purpose is to identify the title. In theory, since each *title* has a specific number and since all publishers submit their serials to the agency assigning ISSNs, the ISSN should be all that is required to identify a title. Unfortunately, this is not the case. When a journal undergoes a title change, it should get a new ISSN. Some publishers, however, simply attach the old title's ISSN to the new title. Some publishers do not submit their journals at all to the appropriate authority for the assignment of ISSNs. Therefore, the ISSN is not completely reliable.

Price or Estimated Price

Always state a price that you are willing to pay for the serial. No one has an unlimited budget and, if you leave the price open, the publisher will start your subscription no matter what it costs. You could find yourself paying several hundred dollars for a serial that you thought cost $15. When you include a price, you indicate to the publisher or agent the price you are willing to pay. If the actual price is greater—most suppliers allow a 10 percent leeway—the agent or publisher will usually contact you to get your permission to start the subscription. If this does not happen, you can always try to cancel the subscription because the actual price exceeded the expected price.

Place and Publisher

The place and publisher helps to identify the title and helps your order department direct the order to the correct publisher. Having this information on the order slip also gives you quick access to the publisher's address in case you have problems later and need to contact the publisher.

Purchase Order Number

The purchase order number is a unique number assigned to each order by the library staff. It can be used to identify the order in case of a problem. Sometimes, simply quoting the **purchase order number** to the supplier enables quick access to your file.

Date of Order

Recording the date on which the order was placed enables you to anticipate when you might receive the serial. We usually allow a couple of months to pass before we begin to worry about the subscription. This time lag varies considerably. Your library management will have its own policy regarding when to begin investigating the "non-receipt" of a new serial.

Your Library's Shipping and Billing Address

Both the shipping and billing address are required. These addresses help the vendors determine where they should send the bills and where they should send the actual serials. In many cases, these two places are the same—you want the serial and the bill to go to the same place. However, in many city libraries, or university and college libraries, the billing may be handled in a central unit while the serial goes to a specific branch.

Supplier's Address

If you get the serial from a source other than direct from the publisher, note this information on the order slip itself. This will help you identify whom you should contact in case there are any problems.

Account Number

There are many different accounts in a library—capital, monographs, retrospective, periodicals, serials, etc. To ensure that the money for this serial is taken out of the correct budget line, include the account number information on the order slip itself.

"Order to Start" Date

In many cases, you do not want the serial to start immediately. You may wish to start the serial with the beginning of the new year or at the start of a new volume. In these cases, you must state when you want the order to begin. This can be either a date (e.g., Order to start January 1996) or a volume (e.g., Order to start with volume 6). This is especially important when you are changing suppliers. Your old subscription will usually continue until the end of the year and you want the new subscription to start with the new year. Unless you specify when the order should begin, you could be receiving duplicate issues for several months. Always include an "Order to start when" date even if it is simply "Order to start immediately."

Edition Wanted

Many publishers are printing more than one edition of a serial, for example, a Canadian and an American edition, or Braille editions or large print editions. If a serial features more than one edition, state the edition that you want. The verification tools discussed in Chapter 2 can help you to determine if more than one edition is offered.

Format Required

Serials are available in microfiche and microfilm as well as CD-ROM, electronic, and paper, so it is necessary to state the format required. The default is a paper copy, but even if this is the format wanted specify it somewhere on the order.

Number of Copies Required

In most cases, you will be ordering only one copy. However, if serials are handled in a central unit, and there are several branch libraries, the library system might be ordering more than one copy. The number of copies wanted, even if it is only one, should always be stated on the order to avoid confusion.

The Requester's Name or Initials (Optional)

The library staff member who initiated the order will usually want to see the serial when it arrives. To make this easier for the serials unit, it is best to include this person's initials on the order form itself.

Special Instructions

Special instructions can vary from library to library. For example, your library might subscribe to a serial designated only for staff use.

On the order form you might note: "For staff use only. Do not process." This message is not for the vendor but for your library staff.

TYPES OF ORDERS

In most large libraries a variety of methods are employed in ordering order serials, each appropriate in a given set of circumstances.

New Subscription Orders

Direct Purchase

A **direct purchase** order means that someone from the library itself has contacted the publisher and set up the subscription. There are several ways to order directly.

1. If the publisher is nearby or has a toll-free number, you can call in your order. This is fast, but you should follow up with an official paper copy of the order to protect yourself in case a problem occurs. Note on the order form that this is not a new order but simply a confirmation of one that has already been placed (e.g., To confirm telephone order of [date]).
2. You can order by mail. Most libraries have a standard letter or official purchase order form. These forms or letters are efficient and easy to use since you simply fill in the blanks with the information necessary to place the order. These orders can also be submitted via fax or e-mail. Following are examples of a form letter (Figure 3.1) and an order slip (Figure 3.2).
    A form letter is, in fact, a letter to the publisher requesting a new subscription. Some libraries create a generic form letter that can be used for all orders, serials, monographs, etc. You simply fill in the blanks. If an item on the form is not relevant or not known (e.g., if you do not know the ISSN), you simply leave it blank. An order slip is just as useful as the letter and it can be used for any type of order.

*** PURCHASE ORDER ***

Publisher's Name: Date: November 5, 1998
Address:
Country: Order no: 0241-15
Postal Code: Account no: 0241-1701

Our library would like to order the following title(s):
Title...........Journal of early adolescence & suppls.
ISSN............0272-4316
Edition.........
Year............start order with January 2002
Place & pub.

Copies..........1 (one)
Unit price.....88.92USD
Total..........88.92USD

Ship to: Small Branch Library,
                 Big Library's Name,
                 Address,
                 City, State, ZIP code
                 Phone number:
                 Fax number:

Invoice to: Main Branch,
                 Big Library's Name,
                 Address,
                 City, State, ZIP code
                 Phone number:
                 Fax number:

NOTE: THIS IS A NEW SUBSCRIPTION ORDER

PLEASE USE ORDER NO. ON ALL INVOICES AND CORRESPONDENCE

FIGURE 3.1. Sample Form Letter

There are advantages and disadvantages to dealing directly with the publisher:

Advantages

- You do not pay any fee for this service (other than the cost of the subscriptions).
- It is easier to cancel a subscription. You can control when the cancellation is to take place.
- Some publishers will only deal with you directly. Many small publishers will not deal with agents.

Disadvantages
- This process can be very time consuming. You must handle many different renewals at different times of the year.
- Many publishers ignore the individual client. The individual generally has little clout.
- You deal with one or more persons at each individual publisher. It is often more difficult to solve problems when you are dealing directly with the publisher.

Purchase Through an Agent

A subscription agent is an intermediary between the library and the publisher. He or she handles all aspects of securing serials for the library: placing orders, ensuring that items are delivered, handling claims, handling renewals, etc. Most agents do not receive any discounts from the publishers. They make their money on service charges that they pass on to the library.

As with ordering directly from the publisher, there are advantages and disadvantages:

Advantages
- Agents bill you only once or perhaps twice a year. This means that you avoid all of those individual renewals that come throughout the year.
- Serials agents are large corporations. As such, they tend to have more clout than the individual has. When problems arise, the publishers tend to listen more closely to an agent than to an individual.
- They look after claims, renewals, and billing. All of these tasks are extremely time consuming for the library staff to handle.
- You deal with only one person. If problem occurs, you can direct your concerns to one individual.

Disadvantages
- You must pay a fee for this service.
- It is more difficult to cancel an order. Since the agent bills you once a year, he or she may have already renewed a serial that you intend to cancel. Cancellations can take up to two years to take effect.

- Some publishers will not deal with an agent, especially small publishers.
- Service levels may vary; the type of service you receive depends upon the agent's representative.

Many libraries will deal with more than one agent. Agents tend to stake out geographical areas. One agent may specialize in British or European serials or in American serials. Another may handle German or Slavic serials. Talking with serials staff in other libraries (and your

---

Library name:

Library address, etc.:

PURCHASE ORDER   Order date: Order valid until:

Order number: Please quote order number on all correspondence.

ISBN/ISSN: Quantity: Unit Price: Format:

Author:

Title:

Publisher: Year: Edition:

Place: Volume:

Name of supplier to whom the order is sent:

      Special instructions:

Customer number: Our fund number:

Ship to:

Bill to (if different from above):

FIGURE 3.2. Sample Order Slip

own experience) will help you to determine which agents are good for which serials. Dealing with more than one agent requires accurate record keeping regarding which agent supplies which title. A misdirected inquiry can mean a long delay in the resolution of the problem.

Memberships

Quite often organizations such as historical or genealogical associations will include their journals as a part of the **membership** package. You become a member of a society or organization and, as a member, you receive the society's publication. In some cases, with one membership you may receive several serials. Agents often will not handle memberships. Generally, it is better to order memberships directly from the association unless you acquire many serials this way. When problems arise, the association will deal more readily with the individual member than with an agent.

When you order a membership, you should use the proper membership form and treat the membership as your subscription. However, you must keep a record indicating which serials are covered by which membership. In some cases, you can order a serial directly from the publisher without acquiring a membership. The cost of the journal ordered this way may, however, exceed the cost of a membership.

Exchanges

Basically, two types of exchanges are used by libraries: a formal arrangement and an informal, occasional exchange. Both can be very useful in obtaining serials.

Formal exchange. In a formal exchange, two or more libraries agree to exchange material on a regular basis. Your library, for example, might be receiving two copies of a report that another library would like to have. You send the other library a copy of the report and, in exchange, staff there send you an item they receive in which you are interested. Exchanges can be very productive. Many exchanges are arranged with libraries in other countries. In fact, exchanges are an excellent means of acquiring smaller, less popular European or African serials.

However, several problems occur with formal exchanges:

- The exchange works only if both parties uphold the agreement.
- It may be difficult to claim missing issues. If the library fails to send a copy of the promised serial, one must be very tactful in "claiming" the missing issue.
- The exchange can work only as long as you have something to offer. If you cancel your order for the item that you exchange, you must find something else to exchange or cancel the exchange agreement.

Informal exchange. An informal exchange is based on choosing items from an exchange list. Often library staff will prepare a list of material that they want to weed. This list is sent to other libraries where personnel identify items on the list that they would like to have. Usually the only charge involved is the cost of shipping.

This type of exchange is not good for current serials. You are unlikely to find any current serials listed since libraries usually discard noncurrent copies only. This type of exchange is excellent for collection building, however, in that it allows you to acquire missing issues. You should act as quickly as possible whenever you receive an exchange list as many other libraries are experiencing the same collection-building process.

Donations

Donations are another excellent way of acquiring certain serials. You can contact the local historical or genealogical society to see if the society would like to donate a copy of any of its publications to the library. Emphasize that this would guarantee an available copy for public use and that the copy will be preserved. Many societies are willing to donate copies of their publications to local libraries.

Standing Orders

Standing orders resemble subscriptions in that you place an order once and the items ordered should continue to arrive until the order is canceled. The difference between a subscription and a standing order is that a subscription applies to a specific serial title while a standing order includes a range of items. A standing order could include everything produced by a particular publisher or everything in a particular series or all items in a particular field of interest. You could have a standing order with the Harleaian Society if you want to receive everything published by that society, or you could have a standing order for only the *African Historical Dictionary* series from Scarecrow Press.

Government Documents

Serials form a large part of the government documents available. They can also be the most problematic of serials to acquire and to manage. Some library personnel have decided, for a variety of valid reasons, that it is not worthwhile to actively acquire government serials.

Free Journals

Several publishers offer their journals free of charge. These could be either in paper format or, as is becoming more popular, in electronic format. Free **electronic journals** can be accessed through the Internet at no cost. All a library needs is the appropriate computer equipment and Internet access. However, even with a free journal, you must consider all of the criteria that we examined when discussing journal acquisition. If the journal does not meet your criteria, do not acquire it simply because it is free.

For electronic journals, consider one more very important criterion—the journal's publisher. Almost anyone with access to the Internet and with some knowledge of html programming can start a new journal. Therefore, a person with no knowledge of medicine could produce a medical journal. It is unlikely that such a person would begin a print version of this journal because of high start-up costs; however, it can be done quite simply and cheaply through the Internet. Be especially careful in selecting any free journals.

Retrospective Orders

Retrospective orders—the acquisition of ceased serials or for non-current issues of serials—pose their own problems. These orders can include anything from the previous year's volume of a serial to a title that has not been published for many years. Although we consider last year's volumes as still "current," agents and most publishers consider only orders for this year's volumes as current orders. All others are classed as backsets or retrospective orders.

Backsets pose a problem in that they require detective work on your part to gather the information needed for the order such as the title for the years wanted, ISSN, etc. Several of the verification tools mentioned earlier include some historical information. Agents' catalogs can often supply the necessary information.

Given the problems inherent in ordering paper copies of backsets, it is often more effective and efficient to order them on microfilm. Most verification tools will state if a serial is available in microfilm or microfiche. These formats are inexpensive and easy to acquire. Although fiche and film are less convenient to use, they are frequently the best means of acquiring backsets.

The retrospective order itself is basically the same as a new order. However, you must be sure to state the actual title that you want and its ISSN. If you supply the wrong title, the order could be delayed or you could be shipped the wrong title. If you want only certain volumes or issues, be sure to state this clearly. It is best to actually list the individual volumes and issues that you want to avoid confusion.

In every library, a combination of serials acquisition methods are used. Some serials will be on direct subscription. Others will come in through an agent. Still others arrive as part of a membership. The serials unit must keep accurate records detailing who supplies which serials. Many other serials functions depend upon our knowledge of the supplier of a particular title.

Chapter 4

Receipt and Check-In of Serials

Objective: Upon successful completion of this chapter, the student will have demonstrated the ability to check in serial issues and to identify common problems associated with the receipt of serials.

PAPER, CD-ROM, MICROFICHE, OR MICROFILM FORMAT SERIALS

Serials arrive at the library in a wide variety of ways. Agents tend to box the library's serials and deliver them in large amounts at a time. Direct subscriptions come in individually on an ongoing basis. Donations come in haphazardly. For convenience, *all* incoming serials should be directed to one area. Items should not be opened by the mail or receiving room staff. Instead, all items should be sent unopened to the person responsible for the receipt of serials. This person will then open all the mail. Wrappers should not be discarded. Instead, they should be put inside the actual issues. If a problem occurs with an issue, for example the wrong title was sent or the issue was damaged, a quick examination of the wrapper will determine if the title was meant for another library or will identify the sender to whom questions can be directed. When the problems have been solved, the wrappers can be discarded.

The serials are often then sorted. Sorting is mainly done with manual serials' systems, which is especially important when more than one staff member is involved in the serials process. The serials should be sorted in a manner that is useful to the library's staff and functions. This could be a strict alphabetical title sort if only one kardex is used. If more than one kardex is used, the initial sort is done and then the serials within that sorting are filed in alphabetical order. Sorting makes the check-in process much more efficient. Automated serial systems require little sorting. Staff simply search for the serial by title and enter the holdings as appropriate. Then the serials are checked in using one of three main means: a holdings list, a manual system, or an automated system.

Because of the ongoing nature of serials, maintaining an efficient system of recording the receipt of serials *as they arrive* is a major component of the work of the serials unit in any library. This information is recorded to let staff and library users know what issues the library has received and, perhaps more important, what has not been received. The most important purpose of a check-in system is to record what is held by the library.

The second purpose of a check-in system is to record any information that helps clarify what has been received by the library. For example, we make a note if the title on an individual issue is different from the main title, or if the numbering system has changed or is wrong, or where a title is shelved. All of this information facilitates access to individual issues and, therefore, should be recorded in the check-in system.

Third, the check-in system can be used to record information of use to both reference and serials staff. This information includes:

- claims made for missing issues;
- renewal notices—when received and when paid;
- name of the supplier (i.e., through an agent or direct);
- index information, such as "Index in vol. 4";
- binding information explaining what, when, and how to bind;
- how many copies are held and which branch or department holds them;
- actual location of the copies in each department or branch (e.g., open shelves);
- weeding schedule, such as "Discard paper copies when film arrives" or "Keep current year only";
- frequency; and
- call number (if applicable).

This is only some of the information that might possibly be included in a check-in system. In fact, library staff can record whatever information is deemed useful.

PRINCIPLES OF THE CHECK-IN SYSTEM

The principles listed here should be followed when checking in serials:

1. The main rule is to enter the information as found on the issue. If the issue has only dates, enter only the dates. Do not invent any other numbering system, such as by volume, that could cause confusion, except in the case of obvious errors (noted in no. 3).
2. Record what has been received. A good check-in system may have added features that provide further information such as claims made, but the basic principle is to record what has been received.
3. If information is missing from a certain issue, and it has obviously been forgotten, supply the information on the kardex in square brackets [ ]. The brackets indicate that the information has been supplied by you. For example, every issue of "X" journal has volume, issue, and date. We have vol. 2 no. 1 1986, vol. 2 no. 2 1986, vol. 2 no. 3 1986, vol. 2 no. 4 1986, but the next issue has only no. 5 1986. Obviously the printer has forgotten the "vol. 2" so we should add it in square brackets [ ]. In this case, we record [vol. 2] no. 5 1986.
4. Enter the date of the publication. In some cases, you may also want to enter the date of receipt. This is usually done only for annuals, but some prefer to enter date of receipt for other serials as well. If you do record the date of receipt, make sure that everyone can identify it as such (e.g., Rec'd April '95).
5. For manual systems, print clearly. If no one can read the information recorded, your efforts are wasted. For automated systems, enter the information in a clear manner so that anyone can interpret the data.

INFORMATION GENERALLY FOUND
IN A CHECK-IN SYSTEM

The following information should be included in any type of check-in system.

1. *Title*
2. *Identifier if the title is ambiguous:* For example, for a serial called *Journal,* you generally include the sponsoring organization's name. Staff at most libraries file entries for ambiguous titles under the name of the organization instead of under the title (e.g., under *Canadian Historical Society. Journal*). Others file ambiguous titles under the title on the title page with the name of the society added, (e.g., *Journal. Canadian Historical Society*).
3. *Call number* (if applicable)
4. *Department or branch location:* This is generally referred to as the primary location.
5. *Location within the department or branch* (e.g., open shelves; history department, open shelves): This is generally referred to as the secondary location. You can also note any patterns in the location. For example, "Current five years on open shelves; earlier in stacks."
6. *Number of copies:* This is especially important if the library receives more than one copy. If so, and if the copies go to different locations, this should be noted.
7. *Source:* How do you get this serial? This indicates whom to contact regarding any problems.
8. *Retention policy:* State which issues the library keeps (e.g., "Current year only kept" or "All issues kept"). If weeding is required, you need to be alerted during check in.
9. *Binding information:* Indicate what you bind and when (e.g., bind every year in March of the following year). You can also indicate the color of binding and spine label required. Having this information on hand eliminates the need to look it up every time you bind.
10. *Frequency of publication:* This is important for claims and binding purposes.
11. *Routing:* If the serial is routed, note who should receive it.
12. *Renewal:* Indicate when the serial was renewed. This helps you to identify which serials have been renewed.
13. *Account number:* Having this on the check-in record will help you when you renew the serial.
14. *Indexing:* Indicate if and where the serial is indexed. Here you would also note if the serial has its own index. This informa-

tion is helpful to the reference staff. Many customers want to know how to find a certain article. If we can tell the customer that every May issue has an index for the preceding year, or that the serial is indexed in a certain periodical index, we can provide better reference service and easier access to the contents of the serial. Also note how you receive the index. Do you need to request it or does it come in automatically? Many indexes must be requested.

15. *Expiration date:* Indicate when a current subscription expires. This will help you identify when to expect a renewal notice.

RECORDING HOLDINGS INFORMATION

As mentioned previously, three ways may be used to record serial information: a holdings list, a manual check-in system, and an automated system.

Holdings List

A holdings list is a record of the issues held by the library, usually arranged in alphabetical order by title. This list could be prepared manually or by using a word processing package such as WordPerfect. If a word processing package is used, the holdings can be easily updated on a regular basis.

A holdings list is simple and inexpensive to prepare. As an issue arrives, the list is updated. Copies of the list should be made available for consultation by staff and customers. The problem with this type of serial recording system is that detailed information usually found in a check-in system, such as routing information, usually cannot be accommodated. "Publishing" all of this information in a list that is available to the public could cause unnecessary confusion as customers attempt to interpret the entries. The library could maintain a detailed list for staff use only or produce two lists: one that contains all the information needed by staff members and a second, simplified version, for the public to consult. Keeping the list current is another problem. As soon as the list is printed, it is probably out of date. To maintain a fairly accurate list, constant reprinting of an updated list is necessary.

Manual Check-In System

In a manual check-in system, serials information is recorded on either stock cards or in a kardex. A stock holdings card is usually a 3" × 5" card, on which boxes have been printed or drawn. These cards can either be prepared in the library or purchased preprinted. If the cards are 3" × 5", they can be stored in a standard card catalog. All the information necessary to identify the serial should be included on the card: call number, title, place of publication, source, purchase order number, fund, and location of the item. This information will often be recorded on one card with a second card listing the holdings attached to the main card.

The information on the cards is generally arranged in the following fashion:

- title and call number are recorded at the top;
- months are listed down the left-hand side; and
- days or weeks are recorded in columns progressing across the card.

As an issue arrives, put a check mark or other easily identifiable mark in the appropriate box to indicate that the issue has been received. For example, the issue of a weekly serial dated the third week of January should be checked off in the January row under the third column. (See Figure 4.1.)

The card in Figure 4.1 depicts a weekly publication. It can also be used for a biweekly publication or even a monthly publication. Identify the month of publication (January, February, etc.), then the week (week one, week two, week three, etc.) and place a mark in the appropriate square. For example, the issue of a biweekly dated the third week of March would be noted in the third square for March.

The card in Figure 4.2 depicts an annual card. Note the years that have been received by the library.

For a monthly publication, use the weekly card and record one entry for each month, or use a monthly card. Figure 4.3 shows an example of a monthly card. Record the year in the left-hand column. In the second column, record the volume (if applicable). As issues arrive, mark in the month received. For example, the January issue will be entered under 01, February under 02, March under 03, etc.

Title					Call no.				
Source					Order no.				
Week	**1**	**2**	**3**	**4**	**5** **Week**	**1**	**2**	**3**	**4**	**5**
Jan.					July				
Feb.					Aug.				
March		√			Sept.				
April					Oct.				
May					Nov.				
June					Dec.				
[Additional information can be entered here]									

FIGURE 4.1. Sample Weekly Stocks Holding Card

The cards illustrated here are useful in a small library where the holdings information can be filed in any convenient location (e.g., the card catalog). This method of recording serials information requires substantial staff time.

Some libraries that use holdings cards to record serials information subdivide their serials into current and noncurrent files. The current file is set up as described previously. The noncurrent file, however, compresses the holdings information. For example, for "Y" serial the library holds issue no. 1, no. 2, no. 3, no. 4, and up to no. 50. Instead of listing each individual issue, the holdings information is compressed to no. 1-no. 50. This form of compression can be used if all issues between the ends of the range are held. Gaps must be identified. For example, with "Z" serial the library has no. 1, 2, 3, 4, 5, 6, 7 up to no. 15 but does not have no. 16; no. 17 to no. 25 are held, but nos. 26, 27, 28 are missing; no. 29 to no. 50 are held. The holdings information can still be compressed, but gaps must be indicated. The holdings are written as:

no. 1-no. 15
no. 17-no. 25
no. 29-no. 50

This information is easier to read if each new "run" of holdings starts on a new line.

Kardex

The most popular manual check-in method for serials is the kardex. Kardex refers not only to the cards on which the holdings information is recorded, but also to the unit which houses these cards. Kardex provides a quick and easy method of recording and retrieving serials information.

The kardex unit itself is a compact cabinet with approximately fifteen drawers. Each drawer can accommodate up to sixty individual kardex cards. Therefore, each kardex unit can hold information for 900 serial titles. Within a drawer, each individual card overlaps the

Title			
Source	Order no.		
Year	**Year**	**Year**	**Year**
1998			
1999			
2000			
2001			
2002			

FIGURE 4.2. Sample Annual Stocks Holding Card

Title													
Source		Order no.											
Year	Vol	01	02	03	04	05	06	07	08	09	10	11	12
2001	24	√	√	√										

FIGURE 4.3. Sample Monthly Stocks Holding Card

next one with only the bottom quarter inch of each card exposed. In this quarter-inch space, the title is recorded. This allows the user to quickly identify the card relating to a particular title.

Depending upon the size of the collection, there could be two or more kardex storage units in use. Some libraries have current serials in one section and noncurrent in another. The units could be subject divided (i.e., one unit for social science, one for literature, etc.) or by type of serial (i.e., a file for government documents and a file for other serials). Library employees devise arrangements that best meet their requirements.

The kardex unit should be placed where all staff—serials staff as well as reference staff—can access it easily. Allow enough work space around the kardex for all the journals being checked in, as well as for other relevant materials such as claim forms. A well-organized work space is essential in a serials unit. If the kardex area is organized for efficient work flow, one person can handle three to four thousand titles in an eight-hour period.

Filing Kardex Cards

Serials staff must be able to locate quickly a certain kardex entry for a particular title. Reference staff members also need to be able to find specific entries quickly and easily. For these reasons, certain conventions have been adopted that make the kardex easy to use.

1. Journals with distinctive titles are filed under those titles. Examples of these are *Maclean's, Newsweek,* or *Rolling Stone.*
2. Journals that have distinctive titles but which have an abbreviation at the beginning of the title are filed under the abbreviation. Examples of these include *RUSI Journal* and *D.H. Lawrence Review.*
3. Journals of academic, historical, or other societies that do not have distinctive titles (e.g., they bear titles such as *Journal* or *Bulletin*) are treated in one of two ways. They can be filed under the title on the title page with the name of the society added. For example, the serial titled *Journal* that is sponsored by the American College of Nutrition would be filed under *Journal. American College of Nutrition.* Alternatively, this serial could be filed under the name of the society and then by the title: *American College of Nutrition. Journal.* Either of these filing conventions is acceptable. However, whichever convention is used must be followed consistently.
4. Memoirs, reports, journals, transactions of societies that deal with the activities of the society, as well as membership lists or progress reports, are filed under the name of the organization. For example, the *Annual Report of the Canadian Historical Association* is filed under *Canadian Historical Association. Annual Report.*
5. Most government documents are filed first by country or political body, then under the issuing body, and finally alphabetically by title. For example, the annual report of the federal Department of Indian and Northern Affairs is filed under *Canada. Department of Indian and Northern Affairs. Annual report.* Many libraries ignore the "Department of" since so many entries fall under this "title." If this is the case, the annual report would file as *Canada. Indian and Northern Affairs. Annual Report.*

These are guidelines only. Library managers establish and follow the practices that work best for them. Whatever filing rules are used, however, must be understood by everyone and be followed consistently.

Recording in the Kardex

There are different ways of checking in items in a kardex depending on the frequency of the serial. The underlying principle is to record information so that the holdings of the library can be quickly identified no matter what the frequency of the serial in question.

1. *Dailies:* Dailies, mainly newspapers, are entered by year and date of issue (not of receipt) by placing a checkmark in the appropriate box (see Figure 4.4). Holidays or other days on which the newspaper was not published should be noted.
2. *Weeklies and biweeklies:* Weekly and biweekly serials are entered by year, volume and issue number or date, as appropriate (see Figure 4.5).
3. *Monthlies:* Monthly serials are entered under the year and appropriate month. Record the information as given on the serial, i.e., if volume and issue are used, record both (e.g., vol. 4 no. 2) (see Figure 4.6).
4. *Bimonthly, Quarterly, and Twice-a-Year Serials:* These are entered in the kardex under the year and appropriate month of publication (see Figure 4.7). For example, if no. 2 of "X" serial is published in March, enter it under March. No. 3 is published in May, so enter this under May. Record the information as given on the serial (e.g., vol. 4 no. 3). Some quarterlies may use the seasons as their numeration. Record this as given on the issue (e.g., vol. 4 fall).
5. *Annuals and Irregular Serials:* Most often these are recorded on a different type of kardex card (see Figure 4.8). The appropriate information is recorded as it appears on the issue. Many librarians also record the date of receipt. This helps predict when the next issue should arrive. If the date of receipt is recorded, make sure that it is clearly labeled (e.g., Rec'd April 15/95).

Source: Copies: Expected arrival:

Location:

Binding information:

Month	1	2	3	4	5	6	7	8	9	10	11	12	13	14	15	16	17	18	19	20	21	22	23	24	25	26	27	28	29	30	31
Jan.	x	x	x	x	x				x	x	x	x	x				x			x	x	x	x								
Feb.																															
March																															
April																															
May																															
June																															
July																															
Aug.																															
Sept.																															
Oct.																															
Nov.																															
Dec.																															

Title:

FIGURE 4.4. Sample Daily Kardex Record

Certain disadvantages to the kardex method include the following:

1. Serials are filed by title only. You need to know the title to find the entry. If only a few words from the title are known, a kardex is difficult to use.
2. The holdings information is not available to the public (unless the kardex is placed in a public area). If customers want to know which issues are held, they must ask a staff member.

Source:	Copies:	Expected arrival:					
Location:							
Binding information:							
Month 2001	Week 1	Week 2	Week 3	Week 4			
Jan.	V. 24, no.1	v. 24, no.2	no. 3	no. 4			
Feb.	v. 24, no. 5	v. 24, no.6	v. 24, no. 7	v. 24, no. 8			
March	v. 25, no.1	v. 25, no.2	not published	v. 25, no. 4			
April							
May							
June							
July							
Aug.							
Sept.							
Oct.							
Nov.							
Dec.							
Title:							

FIGURE 4.5. Sample Weeklies Kardex Report

Source:	Copies:	Expected arrival:					
Location:							
Binding information:							
Month	2000	2001	2002				
Jan.	v. 24, no.1						
Feb.	v. 24, no. 2						
March	v. 24, no. 3						
April	v. 24, no. 4						
May	not rec'd						
June	v. 24, no. 6						
July							
Aug.							
Sept.							
Oct.							
Nov.							
Dec.							
Title:							

FIGURE 4.6. Sample Monthlies Kardex Report

Source: Copies: Expected arrival:								
Location:								
Binding information:								
Month	2000	2001	2002					
Jan.	v. 1, no. 1	v. 2, no. 1	v. 3, no. 1					
Feb.								
March								
April	v. 1, no. 2	v. 2, no. 2						
May								
June								
July	v. 1, no. 3	v. 2, no. 3						
Aug.								
Sept.								
Oct.								
Nov.	v. 1, no. 4	v. 2, no. 4						
Dec.								
Title:								

FIGURE 4.7. Sample Bimonthly, Quarterly, and Twice-a-Year Serials Kardex Report

Source: Copies: Expected arrival:	
Location:	
Binding information:	
Month	
1995	Received May 2/95
1996	Received June 2/97
1997	Not received. Claimed July/97 SM
1998	Claimed June/98 Received July 7/98 SM
1999	Received June 8/99
2000	Received July 3/00
2001	Claimed July 3/01 SM
Title:	

FIGURE 4.8. Sample Annuals and Irregular Serials Kardex Report

Automated System

Library automated systems are becoming very sophisticated. Many libraries now have an automated serials check-in system. Library system vendors have developed serials systems that can be linked to the main catalog. Automating the check-in function has been extremely difficult. No systems come close to being perfect. In fact, some systems cannot function as well as a kardex. An automated system has several advantages:

1. Data can be manipulated to produce a variety of reports. Price increases or the performance of an agent may be studied. Serials that meet a particular criterion can be identified, such as serials that have not been renewed.
2. Information is readily available to the customer. Holdings are listed online in an automated system. This facilitates access and promotes the sharing of resources since libraries can check one another's holdings.
3. All serial functions, such as claiming, renewals, and routing, can be done automatically through the system.
4. Updating records is easy and quick.

Disadvantages include the following:

1. The software is expensive. It can cost up to several thousand dollars to purchase a good serials system. The serials system must interface with the library's catalog, therefore a compatible system must be purchased if one exists.
2. Before you can use an automated system, all the serials information must be converted to machine-readable format. This is costly and time consuming.
3. When the computer is down, you have *no* access to the serials functions. Even when the power goes out, a kardex can be used.
4. You do not see all the information pertaining to a serial on one screen. There is a catalog record screen, a holdings screen, a check-in screen, a claims screen, and perhaps separate screens for problems, renewal, and routing. To get complete information about a serial, all screens must be checked.

5. Training is necessary. It is very costly to train staff to use all of the functions competently. Furthermore, the serials staff now become specialized staff members. It is no longer easy to move staff in and out of the serials unit.

Despite these problems, many libraries are automating the serials functions. Each system is unique but, fortunately, the growth of automation and information sharing has led to the development of standards governing the recording of holdings information for serials.

Guidelines for Recording Holdings

Punctuation for Serials Holdings Statements

Table 4.1 shows the commonly accepted punctuation used in recording holdings:

TABLE 4.1. Commonly Used Punctuation for Serials Holding Statements

Symbol (Name)	Purpose	Examples
: (colon)	Separates hierarchial levels of enumeration and chronology. Also used to indicate supplements or additional accompanying material. No spaces on either side.	1989:Dec. v.24:suppl.
- (hyphen)	Indicates an unbroken range of holdings. No spaces on either side of the hyphen.	Jan. 1960-April 1965
, (comma)	Indicates missing issues that have been printed. No spaces on either side.	1952-1955,1958-1985
/ (forward slash)	Indicates one single physical unit involving two different years or months or volumes. No spaces on either side.	1955/1956
? (question mark)	Is used only as a last digit when the date is unknown.	193?
; (semicolon)	Indicates missing items that were never published. No spaces on either side.	1986-1988;1990-1994
= (equals sign)	Separates alternative numbering. No spaces on either side.	v.3 no. 2=no.10

( ) (parentheses)	Use parentheses when recording chronology along with enumeration or to enclose the title of any index. No spaces on either side of the parentheses.	v.45(1945)
" " (quotation marks)	Use when you record the actual name of the unit being described.	"Updates" "Revised supplement"
[ ] (square brackets)	Use when you supply enumeration or chronology. No spaces on either side.	[2] 2 [i.e. 3]

Guidelines for Coding Serial Holdings Statements in Automated Systems

Many different formats are used for recording holdings information (i.e., a record of what issues the library actually holds). Some are very formal and require extensive training and practice to master. The following format is easy for library staff to use and for the public to interpret and is used in many public libraries. Terms used include **chronology** and **enumeration:**

Chronology: The different types of dates used by the publisher to identify the individual item. This could be simply a month and year, or a day and year, or any variation of dating.

Enumeration: The nonchronological scheme used by the publisher to identify the individual items and to show the relationship of the item to the serial as a whole. The most common are volume, part, or number. Combinations of these are possible also (e.g., vol. 4, part 2).

1.0 Use enumeration and chronology together to record holdings data. Record complete volumes in compressed form with a hyphen to indicate the beginning and the end date of the holdings:
v.1 1980-v.10 1989

2.0 Whenever possible, incomplete volumes should not be compressed. Use a comma to indicate that the library is missing issues for those that have been published but the library does not own. Use a semicolon to indicate missing issues that were not published. Record the issues held; do not record the issues missing.

> v.1 1980-v.10 1989, v.12 1991. (This indicates that the library does not have volume 11 1990 but that it was published.)
> v.1 1980-v.10 1989; v.12 1991. (This indicates that the library does not have volume 11 1990 and that it was never published.)

3.0 *Recording enumeration data.*

3.1 Convert all numeric information to Arabic numbers. For example:

v.VIII	becomes	v.8
First edition		1st ed.
no. five		no.5
Troisième		3e

3.2 For alphabetical data, upper and lowercase characters are recorded as they appear on the publication. Examples:

23a on the issue is recorded as 23a

no.36B on the issue is recorded as no.36B

3.3 Record the captioning used on the issue. Captions should be abbreviated to AACR2 standards, as shown in AACR2, Appendix B. Examples:

volume 5	becomes	v.5
tome 7		t.7
number 3		no.3

If there is no standard abbreviation, use the term given and follow this term by a space such as with *Issue 5* and *Brief 10*.

3.4 When the title carries combined numbering, such as in a double volume (e.g., a physical volume that covers two years), the numbers are separated by a forward slash. An issue that is both volume 1 and volume 2 is recorded as v.1/2.

3.5 Record enumeration data from the highest hierarchial level to the lowest, using a space to separate each level. Some librarians use a colon to separate the different levels. Examples:

> v.1 no.1   v.1 no.1 pt.A   v.1:no.1:pt.ii

The hierarchial order for serials is series, volume, number, month, and date (year).

3.6 For alternative number schemes, in addition to the regular scheme of enumeration, record the alternative scheme following the regular scheme and use an equal sign to separate the two schemes. For example, volume 3 number 1 is also labeled as number 50. This is recorded as:

    v.3 no.1=no.50

3.7   If a title does *not* carry enumeration, do not supply any.

4.0   *Recording the chronological data.*

4.1   When more than one type of date is present, select the preferred date in the following order:

    date of coverage,
    date of publication,
    date of copyright, then
    date of printing.

For reprints, do not record the reprint date. Use only the original date of publication.

4.2   In recording the years, use the following punctuation:

- Use a hyphen to show that the library has all the issues between and including the first date and the last date. Example:

    1969-1979

No punctuation is used following the closing date (i.e., 1979 instead of 1979.).

- Do not use any punctuation if only a single year is held. Example:

    1969

This shows that the library has only 1969.

- Use a forward slash as a separator if the chronology data for a single issue spans a noncalendar year (e.g., an issue covers December 1994 and January 1995) or more than one year (e.g., one issue is published for 1955 and 1956). Do not omit the initial two digits of the second year even if they are omitted on the issue itself. Example:

    Numbering on the item: 1983-1984
    Recorded as: 1983/1984
    Numbering on the issue: 1983/84
    Recorded as: 1983/1984
    Numbering on the issue: Dec. 1994-Jan. 1995
    Recorded as: Dec. 1994/Jan. 1995

- If no chronological data are available, and you can determine a decade but not the exact year, use a question mark to fill the space.
  Incorrect: 1976?
  Correct: 197?
- If the century or decade is not known, the year is not recorded.

4.3 Record months, seasons, and days in the form in which they appear on the publication (romanized if necessary). Data should be abbreviated according to AACR2, Appendix B.

4.4 Record chronology data from the highest level to the lowest. The order is series, volume, number, month, and date (year). Example:
  v.4 no.2 1980

4.5 When more than one calendar scheme is present on the publication, the Gregorian scheme should be used. If the Gregorian scheme is not present, the first calendar scheme cited should be used as the basis for recording the chronology. Convert the non-Gregorian dates to the equivalent Gregorian dates at the highest level only. Example: Chronology on item: minkuo 72 mien 6 yueh 8 is converted and recorded as: 1983

4.6 If a title does not carry chronological data, do not supply it. However, if a serial normally carries chronological data and such data are omitted from a specific issue, supply the missing data within square brackets.

5.0 *Reporting gaps in the collection*

5.1 Indicate gaps in the library's holdings by using a comma: Example: The library has volumes 1, 2, 4, 5. This is recorded as:
  v.1-v.2,v.4-v.5

5.2 Indicate nongap breaks (i.e., items that were never published) by using a semicolon. For example, the library has volumes 1 to 4 and then volume 6. Volume 5 was never published. This is recorded as:
  v.1-v.4;v.6

Guidelines for Recording Holdings: Extent of Unit

When a unit lacks both chronological and/or enumerative information, indicate the extent of the unit, such as 2 CDs or 25 puppets. If the number of parts is not recorded on the unit and if it is not easily determined, record an estimate of the number of units with ca., such as ca. 200 units.

Guidelines for Recording Holdings: Compression

Compressed holdings are indicated by a hyphen -. This shows that the library owns all holdings between and including the first and last part. For example, v.1-v.5 indicates that the library owns volume 1, volume 2, volume 3, volume 4, and volume 5 with no missing parts or volumes.

1.1 If there is no change in the enumeration and/or chronology, compress the holdings at the highest level.
   v.2:no.1(1989)-v.3:no.4(1990) becomes v.2(1989)-v.3(1990)
1.2 If the enumeration and/or chronology differs, compress the holdings for which the enumeration and/or chronology is the same but do not compress any for which the numbering or chronology differs. Leave a space between each element.
   Library owns: v.1(1989), v.2(1990), v.3(1991), v.3:pt.1
   Recorded as: v.1(1989)-v.3(1991) v.3:pt.1
1.3 If the holdings are not complete, do not compress the holdings.

MARC Holdings Information

Holdings information can also be entered into MARC (machine-readable cataloging) holdings according to standards prepared by the American National Standards Institute (ANSI). For serials, we follow ANSI standards Z39.44. There are four possible levels to record the information.

1 and 2. These record very brief information about the holdings, including a brief bibliographic description and the name of the library holding the item.
   3. Includes all information found in Levels 1 and 2 but with more extensive bibliographic information. Also, summary holdings are recorded with open-ended entries often being allowed.
   4. Uses the same process as Level 3 but does not permit open-ended entries.

The actual information to enter does not differ from the standards described previously in this chapter. The basic principle is still to record the information as found on the actual item using the approved abbreviations as found in AACR2. For example, if the item has Band 11 on the cover, record the information as Bd. 11 (note: Bd. is the approved AACR2 abbreviation for Band). If the publisher simply used 5 as the enumeration information, that is all that is recorded—5. Volume is the most popular one for English language material. Volume is abbreviated to v.

The punctuation, chronology, and enumerative information is recorded following the same guidelines discussed earlier. The major difference in recording in a MARC system is the MARC format. All serials holding fields have the subfield $8 to link the information.

There are four main sections of the MARC record in which to record information:

Captions and Pattern (Recorded in Fields 853 - 855)

Here we specify the caption or type of information to be found in the enumerative and chronological fields. The caption describes the manner in which the serial is divided, such as volume or number. We can also record frequency or pattern (e.g., annual) in these fields. Recording the information in these fields is useful in that it will permit the holdings information to be compressed or expanded based on computer algorithms. Think of this as the computer program that will take the information that you provide in the other sections and convert it into a legible product.

All captions and pattern entries begin with the appropriate MARC field number such as 853. The second element indicates if the entries may be compressed or expanded.

0—does not permit expansion or compression.

1—permits compression but not expansion.

2—permits both compression and expansion.

3—unknown (which basically acts as a no. 1).

853 0—this would not permit compression and expanion of the holdings information.

853 1—compression is possible but not expansion.

853 2—the record can be compressed or expanded.

853 3—no information is noted.

The third element in 853 and 854 indicates if the information has been verified:

0—indicates that all information is verified and all levels are present in the actual serial.

1—the captions are verified but not not all levels may be present on the actual serial.

2—the captions have not been verified but all levels are present.

3—no verification of the captions has been done and all levels may not be found on the actual item.

853 13—indicates that compression of the holdings information is possible, but not expansion. Also, there has been no verification of the captions and all levels may not be present on the serial itself.

The 855 field concerns indexes. With an 855 field, the third entry is always 0, which stands for undefined. An $8 element follows: 853 13$8.

Subfields

- $a to $h are reserved for captions that define the enumeration found on the serial. $a to $f represent the different levels of enumeration with $a being the first level to $f being the sixth level.
- $g and $h are for any alternative numbering scheme with $g reserved for the first and $h for the second.
- $i to $m are reserved for chronological captions. The captions indicate the chronology on the actual item. $i to $l indicate the level of chronology with $i being the first and $l being the last.
- $m indicates any alternative chronological scheme.
- $O varies depending upon the field in which it is found. In the 854 it indicates a type of supplementary material such as a publisher's directory. In the 855 field, it is used to indicate the type of index, such as subject or title index, or how often the index appears (e.g., annual). In 856, it indicates the title of the index (e.g., Annual Index or Ten-Year Index).
- $t indicates the copy number (e.g., 1 or 2 or 3).
- $u indicates the number of units in the higher level of enumeration. For example, if the serial is issued in volumes and there are

five parts to the volume, then the number indicated here—in square brackets—would be 5. If there are six numbers to each volume, the number indicated here is 6. When indicating a specific number is useless, use var.

- $v indicates if the numbering system increases continuously—indicated by c—or if the numbering restarts at the completion (e.g., when the volume is complete, the individual parts begin again at 1). This is indicated by r.
- $w is used to indicate frequency: a for annual, b for bimonthly, c for semiweekly, d for daily, e for biweekly, f for semiannual, g biennial, h triennial, i three times a week, j three times a month, k continuously updated, m for monthly, q for quarterly, s for semimonthly, t for three times a year, w for weekly, and x for irregular. When the frequency does not meet one of these preset patterns, then a number is used to indicate the number of issues.
- $x is for calendar month, day, or season in which the higher level ends (e.g., when the volume ends). A four-character code is used: mmdd for month and day. Months are—logically—01-12 and days are 01-31. For example, 0114 is January 14. 0525 is May 25. The seasons are indicated by 21 for spring, 22 for summer, 23 for autumn, and 24 for winter.
- $y is used to indicate the regularity pattern. The specific publishing pattern is set here.
- $z is the type of numbering scheme in use. A six-character code indicates the type of numbering scheme in use. We indicate certain elements:

   First element indicates whether the numbering scheme is numerical (a), a letter (b), a combination of the two with the number first (c), a combination with the letter first (d), or a symbol or other character (e).

   The second element indicates the case in which the information is found (i.e., capital or small letters): a is for no case, b for lowercase, c for uppercase, and d for a mixed case. Script code indicates which script the information is recorded in, such as an for Arabic number and rn for Roman numeral.

   In the case where ordinal numbers are used, e.g., quarterly, then the ordinal number is preceded by a + (e.g., 853 12$81$a (year)$b+qtr.).

Examples of a caption and pattern record:

853 10$8l$av.$bpt.$u4vri(year)$j(season)$wq$x21

In words, this indicates:

1. The records can be compressed but they cannot be expanded.
2. All captions have been verified and all levels of information are present.
3. The highest level is volume with the secondary level being part. There are four parts per volume.
4. The numbering restarts at the commencement of each volume. The new sequence begins in the spring.
5. The first level is indicated as year. The second is season.

853 00$8l$a(year)$w4

1. The information cannot be compressed nor expanded.
2. The captions have been verified and all levels are present.
3. The highest level of the chronology is year.
4. There are four issues per year.

Enumeration and Chronology Fields

The enumeration and chronology fields follow the same guidelines as shown previously. However, this is where the actual data are entered. There are some changes:

1. The first indicator tells the level of encoding that the library uses:
   # indicates that no information is provided.
   3 is for Level 3 information.
   4 is for Level 4.
   5 is for Level 4 with piece designation with a subfield $p.
2. The second indicator is used to identify the form of the holdings:
   # is used when no information is provided.
   0 is for compressed holdings.
   1 is for uncompressed.
   2 is for compressed with the display of the holdings being derived from the textual holdings field.

3 is for uncompressed with the display of holdings being derived from the textual holdings field.
4 is used to indicate which parts are not published.
3. Subfields $a to $m follow the same pattern established for the captions.

- $n is used for a Gregorian conversion.
- $p is used to record the identification number of a specific piece or unit. This generally is a bar code or an accession number. This designation may be preceded by a B for bound or U for unbound to indicate the physical status of the piece.
- $q refers to the condition of the piece. Use this only when the condition being recorded refers to the entire holdings.
- $s can be used to indicate copyright article-fee codes.
- $t indicates the copy number.
- $w is used when there is a break in the holdings. It indicates if the reason for the break is due to incomplete holdings (g) or if no known reason exists for the break (g also). If the break is due to unpublished parts or a lack of continuity, then record n. Basically, if the publisher has published the item and the library does not own it, record g. If the publisher has not published the missing/lacking item, then record n.
- $x is for a nonpublic (i.e., staff) note. Record such things as $xBind when next volume arrives. This is the field in which most library employees will record information regarding supplementary material if the information is for staff use only.
- $z is for a public note, such as $zHoldings incomplete or $zLibrary lacks accompanying workbook.

Enumeration and chronology—Indexes. Index information is recorded in $o, such as $oIndex, which simply indicates that an index is available. Sometimes the information is more exact, such as $oAnnual index found in March issue of following year.

Textual Holdings

Textual holdings are recorded in the 866-868 fields. The use of textual holdings is usually reserved for single-part items. They may also be used for multipart items if the caption and pattern or the enumeration and chronology fields cannot adequately describe the holdings information. Textual holdings may also be used in addition to the caption and pattern or enumeration and chronology fields to record additional information that will generate an additional display.

Indicators. First indicator provides the level of specificity of the enumeration and chronology recorded in the field.

# indicates that no information is provided.
3 indicates that the information is recorded at Level 3.
4 indicates that the information is recorded to Level 4 standards.
5 is used when the information is recorded to Level 4 standards with detailed enumeration and chronology information and an identifying number for the actual physical piece being described in $a.

Second indicator tells the standard used in the holdings:

0 is for nonstandard.
1 is for ANSI/NISO Z39.71 or used if ISO 10324 standards are met.
2 is for ANSI Z39.42.

Subfields. Only a few subfields are used:

- $a is where the actual textual information regarding the holdings is recorded. Example: $av. 2-25(1902-1925).
- $x for nonpublic notes, such as: $av. 2-25(1902-1925)$xBind 2 years together.
- $z for public notes such as $av. 2-25(1902-1925)$xBind 2 years together$zSome larger size issues found in Map cabinets.

Textual holdings are used most often to provide information on supplementary material. You may use this instead of or in addition to the treatment of supplementary materials in caption and pattern or enumeration and chronology. Examples are:

867 30$80$aSupplements to vol. 2-4 (1922-1924) found in 1955 volume.
867 30$80$a456 pieces$zBound in one volume.

Textual holdings may be used to record index information in addition to or instead of recording this information in the caption and pattern or enumeration and chronology fields.

868 30$80$aSeparate index for 1922-1925, then five-year cumulative indexes 1926-1935, then 10-year index for 1936-1945$zNo indexes available for 1946 on.

Electronic Journals

Electronic journals, commonly called e-journals, pose a basic problem for check in. With paper, CD-ROM, microfiche, or film journals, something physical is received by the library staff. We can physically check in the item. However, with electronic journals, nothing physical is received. The vendor simply updates the database to reflect the new edition or new editions, if the database covers several different journals. So, what do we do when we do not receive a physical item to check in? Here are two options:

1. Since nothing physical is received, nothing is recorded. So, the record for an electronic serial, in contrast to most serial records that note what the library actually holds, will simply indicate that the library has this serial starting in [start date]. For example: "Library has from 1995 on." What issue the "on" actually refers to is not stated in the holdings. However, we can generally check this since most electronic journals offer some bibliographic control that allows us to access an electronic file that indicates the issues "published." This, in effect, acts as a check-in screen.

2. Record the issues as they are updated online. This is possible, but someone must check the journal on a regular basis to verify the updates. This alone is time consuming, in addition to the constant updates to the holdings record.

Since we can generally check the actual issues available in an electronic journal, most library personnel tend not to duplicate the work with a further check-in in the individual library. Instead, they favor option number 1.

Chapter 5

Cataloging

Objective: Upon successful completion of this chapter, the student will have demonstrated the ability to catalog a serial according to the *Anglo-American Cataloguing Rules,* Second Edition, 2002 Revision, and identify alternatives to cataloging serials.

PROBLEMS WITH THE FULL CATALOGING OF SERIALS

Many people think that every item in the library's collection should be fully cataloged. Serials have always been the exception to this principle. Few libraries have their serials fully cataloged. In fact, many libraries do not have their serials cataloged at all. Others compromise and catalog annuals that are kept and leave uncataloged periodicals that are not retained. Still others provide minimal cataloging for periodicals.

Cataloging a serial is expensive. Whereas a monograph is cataloged once, a serial record must constantly be updated and changed. It is a labor-intensive process. Other points should be considered as well:

1. How will the needs of your customers best be served? If your clients tend to rely upon browsing to find the journal, then you must carefully consider any cataloging of serials.
2. Cataloging serials is time consuming. It is often difficult to find the necessary information. You may need to search several directories and perhaps communicate with the publisher to ascertain even the basic elements of information required in a catalog record.

3. Cataloging serials is an ongoing concern that does not end until the serial has ceased or the subscription has been canceled. Serials change titles on a regular basis. This requires extensive monitoring and constant updating of records.
4. In full cataloging, subject headings are applied. Are these useful for accessing serials?

Many library managers decide not to catalog their serials. However, the need remains to communicate to clients and staff which serials the library owns and which volumes are held. What are the alternatives to cataloging a serial?

ALTERNATIVES TO CATALOGING

Holdings Lists

Holdings lists are exactly what the name implies: lists that indicate which serials are held by the library, or perhaps several libraries. Holdings lists give minimal information about a serial. Generally, the title, place of publication, and the actual volumes held—or at least an indication of which volumes are held, such as "Current year only held"—are provided. In some cases, the publisher's name is included if this information is needed to avoid confusion with other serials. Other items of information that may be listed are: ISSN, previous titles, notes needed for clarification (e.g., Filed with "X" serial; Bound with "X"), and format if not paper (e.g., microfilm, microfiche, CD-ROM).

The great advantage to holdings lists is that they are relatively inexpensive and easy to prepare. They provide library users with a list of the titles owned as well as an indication of the actual issues held by the library. The list can be typed or, more practically, word processed. If prepared with a word processing software package, the list can be updated quickly and easily on a regular basis. The expense of maintaining the list is minimal if the library already has word processing software and computer facilities. In a small library with only a few serial subscriptions, the list could be put on a blackboard and then updated as new issues arrive.

Several disadvantages to this type of holdings list include the following:

1. The conventions followed in recording holdings dates do not convey precise information to the user of the list. For example, the list may state that the library keeps "Current one year only." What exactly does this mean? If it is March 1995, does the library have all issues since March 1994, or does it have only 1995 issues? Holdings could be indicated as v.1- which means that the library has from volume 1 to the present. But what is the present volume? The specific volumes held are not known. Gaps in the collection are usually indicated by square brackets. For example, [v.4]- indicates that the library has from volume 4 to the present, but that volume 4 is incomplete. We cannot determine, however, which issues are actually missing.

2. The list is usually a printed source. Therefore, the holdings information cannot be shared electronically with other libraries. The printed list can be distributed, but becomes quickly outdated, thus restricting interlibrary loan possibilities. Daily reprinting would be needed to guarantee currency.

3. There is no subject access to the list (unless the library provides a secondary list that groups serials by topic). Most people do not search for serials by subject; however, a subject approach can be useful when trying to locate serials that might be of interest to a particular user group. When no subject access is available, clients looking for serials in a specific field must rely on staff expertise.

Union Lists

A holdings list is usually limited to the holdings of one library. The **union list** or union catalog, is a catalog in any medium that lists the holdings of two or more libraries. Union lists are usually limited in some way. A union list can be limited to all of the libraries in a specific geographic area such as *Union List of Serials in Libraries of the United States and Canada*. Union lists can also be limited to a certain type of library. An example of this is *Guide to Periodicals and Newspapers in the Public Libraries of Metropolitan Toronto*. Union lists can also be limited by subject, such as *Union List of Serials in the Social Sciences and Humanities in Canadian Libraries*. Many variations are possible.

There are five main types of union lists:

1. A *single library list* is unusual, but if a library has many branches, a union list could indicate which branch holds which serials.
2. A *local union list* is limited to a locality, for example, the holdings of the libraries in the city of Hamilton.
3. A *regional list* itemizes the holdings in a particular region. An example would be a list of the holdings of libraries in the Regional Municipality of Hamilton-Wentworth.
4. A *national list* is limited to one country, such as a list of the holdings of the libraries in Mexico.
5. An *international list* is not limited to any one country.

These lists can target a specific topic or subject area or include only certain libraries such as public libraries or university libraries. Some lists have multiple limitations such as a list of archaeological serials (subject) in universities (type of library) in Great Britain (geographical area).

Purposes of a Union List

A union list serves four main purposes:

1. *A location guide:* A union list will indicate the titles owned by a library or branch.
2. *A holdings guide:* A union list also indicates which volumes each branch or library holds. This allows us to direct customers accurately to a specific library for the requested serial.
3. *A source of bibliographic data:* Union lists provide some bibliographic data that can be useful for cataloging purposes. However, the extent of this data is limited.
4. *A bibliography of serial literature:* It lists all serials held in a particular geographic area or pertaining to a particular topic. As such, the list is useful for reference purposes and collection development.

Elements in a Union List Entry

An entry in a union list usually contains the following elements:

1. Title proper
2. Uniform title
3. **Corporate body** that publishes the serial (if appropriate)
4. Edition statement (if appropriate)
5. Numeric and/or chronological designation (i.e., holdings)
6. Place of publication
7. Notes (e.g., format notes)
8. ISSN

The union list is usually arranged in alphabetical order based on the title of the serial. The arrangement of information within entries is generally consistent from one union list to another. The first line gives the title (or uniform title for those titles that have variations), the corporate body or society that sponsors the serial (used only if necessary to provide further explanation or clarification of the title), the edition statement (only if there is an edition), and place of publication (usually only the city).

Beneath this the holdings data are usually presented in three columns. The first column indicates the library system or large library that owns the serial. The second column indicates the actual branch or library where the serial is located. The third column lists the holdings.

The following conventions govern the reproduction of holdings information in union lists:

-	indicates that the holdings continue to the present.
- date	indicates that the holdings go from the first date to the second.
[year or volume number]	indicates that the library has incomplete holdings for that volume or year.
;	indicates that the holdings are broken. They begin again with the volume or number that follows the semicolon.
//	indicates that the serial has ceased publication. It is always found at the end of a year or volume number.

no.	indicates number. Most abbreviations used are taken from AACR2, rev.
mf	indicates microfilm.
mfc	indicates microfiche.
cdr	indicates CD-ROM product.
, [comma]	is used to separate the enumerative information (volume) from the chronological information (date).
v.	indicates volume.

The following are examples of how these conventions are used:

1987-	indicates that the library has all issues, 1987 to the present.
v.181-	indicates that the library has all issues, v.181 to the present.
v.[181, 1992]	indicates that the library is missing some issues of volume 181. No indication is given of the actual issues held.
v.[181]-	indicates that the library is missing some issues of volume 181, but that it has all of the issues of volume 182 to the present (indicated by the dash).
[1987-1989]	indicates that the library has 1987 to 1989 but the holdings are not complete for any of the years, 1987, 1988, and 1989.
v.[181]-v.[183]	indicates that the library has incomplete holdings of volumes 181 and 183, but the library does have complete holdings for the volumes in between (i.e., volume 182).
1986-1988; 1990	indicates that the library has 1986 and all years up to and including 1988 (i.e., the library has 1986, 1987, 1988). The library does not own 1989 (indicated by the semicolon), but does have 1990.
v.[181, 1992]-v.182 no.6, 1993//	indicates that the library has incomplete holdings for volume 181. The holdings end with volume 182 number 6, 1993. The double slash indicates that the periodical has ceased publication. The library does hold v.182 no.1 to v.182 no.6.

The use of spaces is much more liberal in the union list than in other holdings formats. Generally, the entry should be arranged in this format:

v.182 no.6, 1989-v.183 no.3, 1990

Following is an example of three entries from a union list. We will use the fictitious city called Dogville (DOG). Dogville has three library branches: Dalmatian (DLM), Golden Retriever (GOL), and German Shepherd (GER). Next to Dogville is Catville (CAT). Catville is much smaller and has only two branches: Persian (PRS) and Siamese (SIA). The third community in this area is Hamsterville (HAM). It is quite small and has one library, the Hamster Memorial Library (HHM). Together, these three library systems produce a union list.

Bird talk. Los Angeles.
DOG   DLM   *v.[6, 1988]-*

Birder's world. Holland, Mich.
CAT   PRS   *v.10, 1987-*
DOG   DLM   *v.1, 1977-*
DOG   GER   *v.[1, 1977]-v.11, 1988.*

Birding (American birding association). Sonoita, Ariz.
CAT   SIA   *v.19, 1987-*
CAT   PRS   *v.[19, 1987]-v.[21, 1989]-*
DOG   GOL   *v.9, 1977-v.11, 1979; v.13, 1981-v.[14, 1982]-*
HAM   HHM   *v.20, 1988-v.22, 1990.*

These entries are interpreted as follows:

1. *Bird Talk* is published in Los Angeles. Only one library has a copy of *Bird Talk,* the Dalmatian Branch of Dogville Public Library. The Dalmatian Branch has an incomplete set for v.6, 1988, but has complete holdings since then. This branch is still receiving this periodical.
2. Three libraries own *Birder's World.* This periodical is published in Holland, Michigan. To avoid any confusion with a Dutch pe-

riodical of the same or similar title, the state is included (Michigan). The Persian Branch of Catville Public Library has a complete set of *Birder's World* from v. 10, 1987 to the present. The Dalmatian Branch of the Dogville Public Library has a complete set starting with v. 1 in 1977. The German Shepherd Branch of Dogville Public Library has this serial since v. 1, 1977. However, it does not have a complete set of volume 1. The branch also has stopped receiving this periodical with v. 11, 1988. In other words, the German Shepherd Branch has an incomplete set of volume 1 and a complete set from volume 2 to volume 11.

3. *Birding* is published in Sonoita. Most people do not know where Sonoita is, so the state is also included (Arizona). Since *Birding* is the official journal of the American Birding Association, the association's name is included. This inclusion of the society's name is optional except in cases of vague titles (e.g., *Journal*). Two branches of Catville Public Library receive *Birding*. The Siamese Branch has all issues starting with volume 19, 1987 to the present. The Persian Branch has been receiving the periodical since volume 19, 1987. It does not have a complete set for volume 19, 1987 nor for volume 21, 1989. The branch does, however, have all of the other issues and still receives this periodical. Only the Golden Retriever Branch of Dogville Public Library has a subscription to this periodical. Its holdings begin with volume 9, 1977. It has all of the issues from volume 9 to volume 11 but for some reason does not have any issues of volume 12, 1980. The collection begins again with volume 13, 1981. The branch does not have a complete set of the issues for volume 14, 1982 but does have all of the issues since then. It still receives *Birding*. The last library to have this serial is Hamsterville's Hamster Memorial Library. It has all issues from volume 20, 1988 to volume 22, 1990. It does not currently receive this periodical.

Brief Entries in an Online Catalog

Instead of including complete catalog records for serials in the catalog, libraries often provide brief records. The level of detail included in these brief records varies from one library to another. Some libraries provide the title, publisher, and place of publication in the catalog record. Others provide these elements plus basic subject access, such as *Africa—Periodicals*. Library personnel customize the catalog record to accommodate the needs of their clientele.

You can also customize the level of information provided about the holdings. You can list each issue held, or you can simply provide a summary statement of what is held, such as v.4 1972- . This indicates that you have all issues from volume 4, 1972 to the present.

Online records and holdings can be updated quickly and easily. Updated information is available immediately to the catalog user. If your catalog supports dial-up access or is available on the Internet, other libraries can examine your serial holdings. This facilitates resource sharing through interlibrary loan.

Public Access to Check-In Records

The library can make its check-in records, kardexes, stock cards, or other check-in systems available to the public. The great advantage in providing this type of access is that the information is already available. No extra cataloging or holdings list preparation is necessary. Customers have access to up-to-date records that show a great deal of information about the serials owned and the actual volumes held in the collection.

Several disadvantages in providing public access to check-in records include the following:

1. Security of the holdings data could be compromised. If the public is allowed access to check-in records, someone could potentially change information found in the records.
2. Providing this type of access would slow the check-in process. Often we write cryptic notes to ourselves or to the other staff members. These notes are familiar to us so we can interpret them easily. However, if we open our check-in systems, the notes as well as the holdings information will need to be clear and easily understood.
3. The volume of information in a check-in record may be overwhelming or confusing to some customers.

Opening the check-in system to the public may not be a realistic alternative for all libraries, but for a private or small specialized library, it might work well.

CATALOGING SERIALS

In deciding whether to catalog its serials, a library staff must consider:

- *Needs of customers:* If your public is highly computer literate and relies heavily on the online catalog, you may wish to catalog serials to provide online access. This is especially true if users access the catalog from remote locations.
- *The library's mission and goals:* If providing online access to all materials in the library is one of the library management's goals, then serials should be cataloged and included in the library's catalog.

Advantages to cataloging serials include the following:

1. Access to serials is enhanced by providing title access, and perhaps subject access.
2. Serials can circulate in an automated circulation system. A record for an item must be in the database before that item can circulate. Cataloging provides this record.
3. The library customers' self-sufficiency is promoted. In an online system, customers have access to the complete serial record including the bibliographic screen, the holdings screen, the check-in screen, etc.
4. The sharing of information is facilitated. Once serials are listed in the online catalog, other libraries have access to the library's holdings. This facilitates resource sharing and interlibrary loans.
5. The actual holdings can be made available online. You can put holdings online only if you have a record to which you can attach the holdings.

Once a library staff decides to catalog its serials, the next question to ask is: what level of cataloging will be done? If your goal is to make holdings information available to your customers, perhaps a basic catalog record (title and publisher) to which you can attach the holdings information will be sufficient. If you plan to act as a resource for other libraries, you may need a more detailed catalog record. AACR2 describes three levels of cataloging and variations within these three levels. The *first* and most basic level consists of the following elements:

- *Title proper:* Record the chief title of the serial, including alternative titles, but not any parallel titles and subtitles.
- *Statement of responsibility:* You record only the first name given as the person responsible for the content of the item.
- *Edition statement:* If applicable, provide edition such as Canadian, Braille.
- *Holdings statement:* Indicate which department or branch holds the title.
- *Imprint:* You record only the first publisher listed. You also record the date the serial began publication, but not the place of publication.
- *Extent of the item* (i.e., how many volumes are in the complete run of the serial): You always state this as volumes or v. even if the serial uses numbers. For example, if the serial uses no. 1, no. 2, no. 3, etc., you still record *v.* in the extent of the item. You record the number of volumes *that have been published,* not the number of volumes held by the library. So, for example, the library has only two volumes of the fictitious *Scott's Annual Review,* which has ceased publication. In all, it was in publication for twenty-four years. The physical extent of the item would be 24 v. even though the library owns only two volumes. The library's actual holdings can be listed in the holdings record. For serials that have ceased, you can actually state the extent of the items, such as fifty-two volumes. For serials that are ongoing, we do not know how many volumes will be published. We simply note *v.* to indicate that there are volumes; how many is not known.
- *Series statement:* A series statement is added only if it is important. Generally the series statement is omitted but, if you decide that series information is important to your clientele, you should include it.

- *Notes:* Include any notes of importance. These notes could concern shelving arrangements (e.g., Shelved with "X"), frequency (e.g., Quarterly, Annual), etc.
- *ISSN (International Standard Serial Number):* This is a unique number assigned to each serial to identify it.

The *second* level includes all of the previous with the following additions:

- *Title:* The title information also includes parallel titles and subtitles *if they are deemed important.* After the title proper, the general material description may be given (e.g., microfilm) but this is optional.
- *Statement of responsibility:* All statements are given.
- *Place of publication:* Only the first place listed is given for serials.
- *Extent of item:* This includes other physical details such as dimensions.
- *Series statement:* This is given for the main series only.

The *third* level includes all of the elements mentioned in AACR2 that are applicable to serials. It also includes *all* title information such as all parallel titles and subtitles, all statements of responsibility, all series statements, including subseries, etc. You can adapt the record to meet your own library's needs by including notes such as locations, holdings, etc. Most libraries use the first level but modify it to suit the needs of their clientele. One major modification is that most libraries do include the publisher and place of publication in the catalog record.

Once the library staff has decided on the level of cataloging appropriate for the serials collection, the next question to ask is: How will the cataloging be done? Will library staff members do the cataloging themselves or will the library purchase cataloging services? Many libraries buy their cataloging from a vendor and then adapt it to meet their needs. The question of buying cataloging or doing it ourselves really depends on the extent of the serials collection and the level of cataloging needed. If you have only a few serials and need basic cataloging, you can probably catalog the serials inhouse. If you have an extensive collection and/or want to provide detailed catalog records, you may want to purchase the cataloging.

Data Elements Necessary to Describe a Serial

Certain elements of information must be included when cataloging serials:

1. *Title and statement of responsibility:* You need to record the title proper and the statement of responsibility.
2. *Edition statement* (if applicable): If you have a Braille edition or an American edition, etc., this must be indicated. If no edition is given, do not create one. Record only what is given on the serial itself.
3. *Numeric/chronological designation from the* first *issue:* Record the numeric or chronological designation as stated on the first issue of the serial. **Numeric designation** (also knows as **enumerative designation**) refers to the numbers used to identify the issue (e.g., vol. 4 or issue 5 or vol. 4 no. 6). The **chronological designation** refers to a date (e.g., Jan. 1995 or Jan. 15, 1995).
4. *Publication information:* Who publishes this serial? Record only the first name given. Record also the first place of publication listed. Often you will find that the place of publication is listed as Amsterdam, New York, London, Toronto, Delhi. Always record only the first place listed, in this case, Amsterdam.
5. *Physical description* (if noteworthy): This is generally recorded for serials that are *not* in paper form. Therefore, the physical description usually refers to the format of the serial such as film, fiche, or CD-ROM. Also, record the extent of the item. For serials that have ceased publication, state the number of volumes published. For ongoing serials, simply record *v.* to indicate that the number of volumes that will be published before the serial ceases publication is unknown.
6. *Series:* If the series information is important in the judgment of the cataloger, it should be included.
7. *Notes:* The notes field contains such information as the frequency of publication, the source of the title information if it was not taken from the chief source of information, the issuing body, and the editor. The issuing body and the editor are recorded only if this information is considered to be important for the user of the catalog record. All of these points will be discussed in more detail later.

8. *ISSN:* The ISSN must be included in the catalog record. If an ISSN cannot be located on the actual serial, try the verification tools mentioned earlier. If the ISSN is still not found, leave this element blank. Do not create one.

Prescribed Source of Information

As when cataloging monographs, there are certain places to find the information needed to catalog a serial. According to rule 12.0B1 of AACR2, the title page, whether it is published with the first issue or later issues, or the title page substitute of the first issue of the serial, is considered the **chief source of information.** In an ideal world, we would always turn to the title page of the first issue of the serial and find all the information needed to create the catalog record. Unfortunately, it is not always easy to find the title page and, in many cases, the first issue does not include a formal title page. Perhaps the graphics were not ready so the formal title page was not included with the first issue. Rather than wait for a title page to be produced and delay the public's access to the serial, use alternatives to the first issue title page.

AACR 2 is quite explicit as to the alternatives that are acceptable and the order in which they should be selected. According to rule 12.0B1, the order is as follows: title page (which is the chief source of information), and, if the title page is not present, the cover, followed by the caption, **masthead,** editorial pages, **colophon,** or other pages. If the information is taken from any place other than the title page of the first issue, this fact must be noted in the notes area of the catalog record.

Each area of the catalog record has an AACR 2-prescribed source to which you should turn for information.

Area	Prescribed Source
Title and statement of responsibility	Chief source of information
Edition	Chief source of information, preliminaries, colophon
Numeric or other form of designation	Same as edition statement
Publication	Same as edition statement
Physical description	The whole publication
Series	The whole publication
Notes	Any source
ISSN	Any source

Access Points

Three "problems" that must be tackled before beginning the actual cataloging are the concepts of main entry, uniform title, and the use of qualifiers to distinguish titles.

Main Entry

Main entry is the lead element in a record. For a monograph, in most cases the main entry is the author. AACR2, Chapter 21, describes how to choose a main entry for serials. A personal author is the main entry if this person is chiefly responsible for the production of the work (rule 21.1A1). Rarely is a serial the work of only one person. Rule 21.6C2 indicates that if four or more authors are involved in the creation of a work, the main entry will be under the title. In most cases, more than four people are responsible for producing a serial (all the contributors, the editors, referees, etc.), serial main entries are usually under title. There are exceptions. If the serial emanates from a corporate body and if more than half of the material contained in the publication deals with the policies or operations, etc., of that body, then the main entry will be under the name of the corporate body. For example, if the serial is a company newsletter and over half of the issue deals with the company's policies, procedures, or activities, the main entry will be under the corporate body. Otherwise, the main entry is under the title.

Uniform Title

A **uniform title** is the title by which a work with a varying title is commonly known. It provides identification for a serial that has many different forms of the title. The uniform title is most commonly used when a date appears in the title of the serial, such as the Australian War Memorial's *Annual Report 1979-80*. Next year, the title is different: *Annual Report 1980-81*. Travel guides that include the year of coverage in the date are another example: *Fodor's Japan 1993, Fodor's Japan 1994, Fodor's Japan 1995,* etc. In these cases, uniform titles are established that consist of the basic titles minus the dates: *Annual Report* and *Fodor's Japan.*

Qualifiers

Qualifiers are used to differentiate two or more serials that have the same title. Consider all the published *Newsletters* and *Journals*. The qualifier is enclosed in parentheses following the title. The first occurrence is cataloged as any other serial. *Only the second and any other serials that share the same title are given the qualifier.*

Generally the place of publication is used as the qualifier. Let's assume that we have a serial called *Currents* in our library. It has been cataloged. We now start to receive a second serial with the same title. The second serial is published in New York City. The entry for the second serial would be: *Currents (New York, NY).* Sometimes the name of the corporate body responsible for the serial is used as the qualifier instead of the place of publication. This is limited to cases in which the title proper consists of words that indicate a "type" of publication—*Bulletin, Newsletter, Journal* or a frequency—*Occasional Papers, Weekly Newsletter.* In either of these cases, if a serial with that same title is already in the collection, we use the corporate body's name as the qualifier. The main entry for the *Newsletter* of the Canadian Thoroughbred Association would be *Newsletter (Canadian Thoroughbred Association)* if the collection already has a serial titled *Newsletter.*

Chapter 12 of AACR2 is devoted to cataloging serials:

Main Entry. The first decision in cataloging a serial is to determine the **main entry.** Follow the directions given previously. Except in a very few cases, the main entry will be the title. As already discussed, one exception is a serial that deals almost exclusively with company policies and procedures. For example, the fictitious *Newsletter* of the *Mohawk College Library Resource Center* deals exclusively with the policies and operations of the library. In this case, the main entry will be under the corporate body Mohawk College Library Resource Centre. The catalog record begins:

Mohawk College Library Resource Center.
Newsletter / issued by the Mohawk College Library Resource
Center.—
No. 1 (Jan. 1993)- .—Hamilton, Ont. : The Centre, 1993-

Title Proper. The next element transcribed will be the title proper. Transcription of the title proper follows the same rules as for monographs (rule 1.1B). However, rule 12.1B7 describes a very important exception to this rule for serials. If the title includes a date or a number and if the date or number is not an integral part of the title, it should be omitted when transcribing the title. The "test" to see if the date or number should be included is to examine several issues. If the date or number is constant for every issue, transcribe the date or number. If the date or number changes for every issue, do not transcribe it. If the date or number is found at the beginning of the title and if it varies for every issue, simply ignore it. If the number or date is found elsewhere, replace it with the marks of omission (. . .). Examples:

Hong Kong Report for the Year 1993
You transcribe: Hong Kong Report for the Year . . .
but *1994 World Fact Book*
You transcribe: World Fact Book

Other title information. AACR2 states that the cataloger should transcribe other title information according to rule 1.1E. However, other title information is not usually included depending upon the individual library. Subtitles can be included as notes if the cataloger deems them important. However, other title information *is* included if a serial bears both an initialism and a full form of the same title in the chief source of information (rule 12.1E1). For example, *Reference Services Review* bears the title *RSR: Reference Services Review.* The catalog record will include both the initialism and the full title.

RSR : reference services review.—Vol. 1, no. 1 (Jan./Mar. 1973)-   .—
Ann Arbor : Pierian Press, 1973-

Statements of responsibility. Generally, you follow the instructions in rule 1.1 F when transcribing the statement of responsibility. Exceptions are described in Chapter 12 of AACR2.

1. Rule 12.1F2 indicates that if the title includes a statement of responsibility or the name of the sponsoring body, a further statement of responsibility is not transcribed unless it appears separately from the title in the chief source of information. In other

words, if the only information on the chief source of information (title page) is *Mohawk College Library Resource Center
Newsletter,* there will be no further statement of responsibility.
However, if the title page gives the title and a separate statement
of responsibility such as "published by the Mohawk College Library Resource Center," then the statement of responsibility is
transcribed.

2. The editor's name is not recorded as part of the statement of responsibility (rule 12.1F3). However, if the cataloger determines
that the editor's name is important, an added entry is made for
the editor and his or her name is indicated in a note (see rule 12.7
B6). The editor's name is never included as part of the statement
of responsibility.

Edition statement. The rules for the edition statement are found in
rule 12.2.

1. Rule 12.2B1 gives a list of situations in which an edition statement must be transcribed:

   • Local edition statements. Certain serials, especially newspapers, have different editions depending upon the locality. For
   example, you could have a Toledo edition, a New York edition, and a Los Angeles edition of the same serial.
   • Special interest edition statements. These are statements that
   indicate that the edition is targeted to a particular user group.
   Examples of these include Children's ed., Medical ed.
   • Special format edition statements. These statements identify
   the format of the serial, for example, Braille ed., Library ed.,
   Microform ed.
   • Language edition statements. In some cases, the same serial
   may be published in several different languages. Examples
   include French ed., English ed., Italian ed.
   • Reprint or reissue statements, or revisions. These statements
   are used to illustrate that the serial in hand is a reissue or reprint; it is not the original. These statements are used only if
   the complete run of the serial has been reissued, reprinted, or
   revised. Examples include Reprint ed., Reissue ed., Rev. ed.,
   2nd ed.

2. Rule 12.2B3 states that if the edition statement appears in more than one language, transcribe the edition statement in the language of the title proper. Optionally and in general use for bilingual Canadian serials, you can record both the French and the English statement and put an equal sign (=) between them to show that they are parallel or equal. As for which goes first, the French or the English, you generally follow the precedent set by the title proper (e.g., if the title proper has English first, record the English edition statement first; if the title proper has French first, record the French edition statement first).

Numerical and/or alphabetical, chronological, or other designation. Rule 12.3 covers the transcription of numerical and chronological designations. This rule is straightforward. Two points should be emphasized:

1. Always start this section of the catalog record with the first issue even if the library does not own the first issue. Record the designation exactly as given on the first issue (rule 12.3B1). You may need to check other sources to determine when the serial began and what designation was given to the first issue. If the first issue lacks any designation but later issues have one, adopt that designation for the first issue and put it in square brackets to show that you provided the information. For example, the serial you are cataloging has no designation on the first issue. However, the second issue bears No. 2, the third No. 3, the fourth No. 4, etc. Therefore, record this numbering system in the catalog record as [No.1]-   . Remember that you are recording when the serial began publication, not when the library started to receive the serial. For example, the library subscribes to the *Mohawk College Library Resource Center Newsletter* beginning with the January 1995 issue. The catalog record for this publication must state when the first issue began (i.e., January 1993, not January 1995). The actual holdings of the library can be indicated in a holdings note.

2. The capitalization of Vol. and v. can be confusing. Capitalize the "v" only when it is the first letter of the first word in each area or part of the record. Examine the following entry:

Reference review.—Vol. 1, no. 1 (Jan./Mar. 1980)-v. 10, no. 4 (Oct./Dec. 1989).—Toronto : Reference Press, 1980-

The first reference to the designation, *Vol.*, is capitalized since it begins a new area. The second and all other designations are not capitalized. Note also that *no.* is not capitalized since it is not the first element of the area in this particular record. The first time that you make a reference to volumes, use *Vol.* For all subsequent references, use *v.* only. See Appendix B of AACR2.

3. Abbreviations used (e.g., v., no.) are all specified in AACR2, Appendix B.

4. Transcribe numbers as instructed in Appendix C of AACR2.

5. Unless the serial has ceased publication, you cannot fill in the ending designation. Since you do not know when the serial will end, after the beginning chronological designation put a hyphen, four spaces, and a period, e.g., No. 1 (Jan. 1993)-   .

6. You record information as given on the serials themselves (rule 12.3B1 and rule 12.3C4). In some cases this can produce confusing entries. For example, consider a serial that began with a strict chronological designation (e.g., January 1984), then changed to a numbering system in 1985 (e.g., January 1985 was No. 1), then in 1987 changed to a volume and number system (e.g., January 1987 was vol. 1 no. 1), and then ceased publication in February 1987 (e.g., vol. 1 no. 2). You still record the information as given on the individual issues of the serial. The designation would be Jan. 1984-v. 1 no. 2 (Feb. 1987).

Publication, distribution, etc., area. The basic rule is to record the first place of publication given, the first publisher listed, and the date when the first issue was published. All other information, such as other places of publication or editors, is not recorded in this area of the catalog record.

When transcribing the name of the publisher, note that if the name is transcribed in the title proper, you record an abbreviated form of the name in the publication area. The *Mohawk College Library Resource Center Newsletter* is published by the Mohawk College Library Resource Center. The name of the publisher is given in the title. Therefore, in the publication area, we record only: The Center. The catalog record for this serial will be as follows:

Mohawk College Library Resource Center newsletter.—No. 1
(Jan. 1993)-　　.— Hamilton, Ont. : The Centre, 1993-

Rule 12.4F governs transcription of the date of publication. This date will be the year as found on the first issue of the serial. Follow this date with a hyphen and then the ending date, if there is one. If the serial is ongoing, follow the beginning date with a hyphen and four blank spaces as stipulated in rule 12.4F1.

Physical description area. Rule 12.5B1 describes how you transcribe the extent of the item. For serials that are currently received or for serials that have not ceased publication, we cannot determine the *full* or *complete* extent of the item. We have no idea how many volumes will eventually be published. For these serials we simply transcribe v. to indicate that there are volumes but that we do not know how many. For serials that have ceased, we can determine how many volumes have been published, and we transcribe the total number of volumes such as 5 v. or 24 v. Two points are worth stressing. Record the number of volumes published, not the number of volumes held by the library. For example, the library's collection may contain only volumes 3, 4, and 5 of a serial that ceased with volume 5. However, in this area of the catalog record, you record 5 v. Use serial directories or other catalogs to determine how many volumes were published. We also record the number of volumes published, not the number of volumes bound. The previous example could be a very slender serial that the library has bound in a single volume. We still record 5 v. in the physical description area.

Illustrations can be noted as indicated in rule 12.5C. Usually, the presence of illustrations is noted only if the serial has a large number of illustrations as an art or fashion periodical might.

The size of the serial is usually based on the average size of the individual issues. Generally, the size of the issues does not change. However, if individual issues are larger than any others and this is seen as a potential problem (such as for shelving or for retrieval), then the irregularities can be mentioned in the notes field (rule 12.5D).

Accompanying material is recorded only if it is issued regularly with the serial (rule 15.5E). For example, note if a serial regularly includes microfiche along with the print serial. If the microfiche are issued haphazardly, their presence is not recorded in this area of the catalog record. Frequency is not noted in the physical description area (rule 12.7B11). Rather, it is indicated in a note.

Series. The series area is generally used only for scholarly serials (rule 12.6). The rules that govern transcription of the series statement are basically the same as for monographs.

Notes area. This is one of the most important areas of a serial record because of the variety and extent of notes possible. General instructions for notes are given in rule 1.7A. Notes that pertain specifically to serials are covered in rule 12.7A.

The principal notes used for serials are:

- *Frequency* (rule 12.7B1): AACR2 states that you should give the frequency unless it is apparent from the title of the serial, for example, *Wildlife Quarterly*. In most libraries, the frequency is given even if it is indicated in the title. Also, state any variations in the frequency such as Three issues from Jan. 1978-May 1985; quarterly from June 1985-Sept. 1985; annual, Oct. 1985-.
- *Source of information* (rule 12.7B3): If the chief source of information is not the title page, note the source of information used in a note. The generic phrase is Title from and then the source such as Title from cover.

  Certain sources are accepted for obtaining serial information. These include all of the directories discussed previously as well as union and library catalogs and statements of ownership. A statement of ownership is published in a serial and provides basic information about the serial (title, issuing body, frequency, ISSN) as well as the number of issues produced. American serial publishers are required by law to include a statement of ownership once a year in each serial. Unfortunately, these statements are often difficult to find. You may search several issues of the serial before you locate one. The statement of ownership is, however, one source in which the information needed for a catalog record is generally brought together.
- *Statement of responsibility* (rule 12.7B6): Make any notes that are needed to expand on or clarify the statement of responsibility. You have much more freedom here than you do in the actual catalog record itself. You can include a statement of responsibility that is not acceptable in the statement of responsibility area. For example, *ACRL News* is published by the American Library As-

sociation. That organization will be transcribed in the statement of responsibility area. However, this serial is issued by the Association of College and Research Libraries. This issuing body can be mentioned in the notes area as Issued by: Association of College and Research Libraries. The most frequent use of the notes area is to identify editors of importance. For example, if Margaret Atwood edits a serial, we cannot include her name in the statement of responsibility. However, it is important to note that she is the editor in the notes field: Editor: Margaret Atwood.

* *Links with other serials* (rule 12.7B7): This type of note links two or more serials. In most cases, the link is needed to indicate a title change. The most commonly used linking notes are Continues: and Continued by:. Continues links the new title to the old title and Continued by links the old title to the new title. Another significant linking note is Supplements. The existence of supplements is noted here, for example, Supplements accompany some numbers or Supplements issued every Sept.
* *Notes on numeration or chronological designation* (rule 12.7B8): Notes about variations in numeration or chronological designation such as irregular numbering are placed here, for example, First issue unnumbered, Suspended June 1976-Jan. 1978. Notes are recorded in a particular order. See rule 12.7B in AACR2.

Standard number and terms of availability area. Generally, the last element included in a serial record is the ISSN. This is transcribed as ISSN xxxx-xxxx. You can also state the price here such as $10.00 per year (rule 12.8D). Most libraries do not include the price in the catalog record because the price changes so often. The following is a typical serial record with standard punctuation and spacing.

Title proper [general material designation when required; depends on library policy] = parallel title(s) if required / first statement of responsibility.—Edition statement.—Numeric and/or alphabetic or other designation.—First place of publication : first publisher, date of publication.
Extent of item : other physical details ; dimensions.—(Series. Subseries)
Notes
ISSN

CATALOGING INTERNET SERIALS

The main question concerning Internet serials is why catalog them at all? Many library personnel have decided not to. They simply offer them on an Internet terminal with signage indicating which e-journals are available. The e-journals are not cataloged. The advantage to this type of approach is that changes (updates, addition of new titles, discontinuation of others) have little or no impact on the staff and the library's customers. The disadvantage is that there is no indication in the library's catalog of which electronic journals are available. Unless customers seek help from library staff they may never know that potentially relevant material can be accessed electronically. Indeed, they might conclude that the very titles they are seeking are not available.

So, for some libraries, the only solution to this dilemma is to catalog serials available though the Internet. This provides subject and title access to the journals. In effect, this would mean that the customer can jump from the library catalog to the actual e-journal itself with no difficulty (assuming a hypertext link is provided).

Other reasons to catalog e-journals include:

1. An immense amount of material is available through the Internet. Not cataloging items of use to us would be comparable to not cataloging the monographs in your library.
2. Internet resources do need to be organized in some manner. By providing catalog records and subject headings, we begin to exert a degree of control over the massive amount of material available.
3. Providing the hypertext link in the catalog record is the most efficient method of accessing Internet resources.

Chapter 9 of AACR2 includes provisions for the cataloging of computer files available through remote access. In contrast to this are files that are accessed through direct access or carriers such as disks, cartridges, or cassettes that are inserted into the computer. Internet resources obviously fall under the "remote access" category.

The following guidelines describe how to catalog an Internet serial. These guidelines address only the special problems posed by cataloging items available through "remote access."

- *Chief source of information* (AACR2 9.0B1): The chief source of information is the title screen or a printout of this screen. If no title screen exists, the information can be taken from the "readme file," the "about" screen, documentation file, internal menus, labels, subject lines, program statements, etc. If no information is provided, the information supplied on the home page is adequate. If no title information is given, a file name may be used if available. If nothing is provided, the cataloger must supply a title.
- *General material designation* (AACR2 9.1C): The GMD is almost always "computer file." This information is provided immediately following the title proper, enclosed in brackets.
- *Edition statement* (AACR2 9.2B): If the file contains any words to indicate that another edition exists or that the same information was provided in another earlier format, that word or phrase is treated as an edition statement. Examples of this include Electronic version, Working draft, ASCII ed. (The last indicates that there may be a version in another format.)
- *File characteristics area* (AACR2 9.3): This includes two parts: the designation and the number of files or records. The designation is limited to one of the following: Computer data, Computer program, Computer programs, Computer data and program, or Computer data and programs. The number of records is not used in serials unless the serial is complete and the size of the file could be determined (e.g., Computer data [1 file : 23456 bytes]).
- *Publication, distribution, etc. area* (AACR2 9.4): In the interest of simplicity, all items on the Internet are considered as published. Therefore, a place, publisher, and date will be provided in the catalog record unless nothing is indicated. If nothing is indicated, use s.l. and/or s.n. as appropriate.
- *Physical description* (AACR2 9.5): This area is omitted since no physical item is being cataloged.
- *System requirements* (AACR2 9.7B1b): This note indicates what computer is required, how much memory is needed, and if any other programs are needed to run the file.
- *Mode of access* (AACR2 9.7B1c): The Internet is the mode of access. Most commonly the phrase used is Mode of access: Internet, but others are also available, such as Access through computer network or Electronic access through Internet. Also

at this stage, you can provide the host name and address (e.g., Mode of access: Internet. Host: http://www.myowntitleplacedhere.com).

- *File characteristics* (AACR2 9.7B8): Provide here further information about the file that is not recorded elsewhere. This could include conversion notes, tagging information, or the format of the actual file itself.
- *Copy being described, library's holdings, restrictions on use* (AACR2 9.7B20): Indicate here any note on library holdings. For example, different date ranges could be covered in different files (e.g., file one covers 1990-1995; file two covers 1995-1999). The library staff may, for whatever reason, decide to provide access only to the second file. The library holdings note would therefore indicate that only the second file was available. Also, any restrictions on use are noted here. The most common one is a note indicating that access is only available in the library (and not by remote access). Notes about purging the files can also be put in here (e.g., Destroy September 1).

CATALOGING STANDARDS

AACR2 establishes cataloging standards for all libraries. By adhering to these standards, we ensure that we all catalog in the same manner. Therefore, regardless of which catalog we use to search for a particular item, the catalog record retrieved will be essentially the same. Variations may occur in the level of cataloging detail provided, but the basic components of the record are consistent.

The establishment of these standards has been a blessing for library staff and customers. Once the standards are understood and followed by everyone, we can effectively share information about serials. We can examine any record and know exactly what each item of information means.

Take, for example, the case of *Wiez*. A customer comes to the serials information desk for help with this word. By itself, it means absolutely nothing (unless you happen to understand Polish). Is it a title? a publisher? a place of publication? volume in Polish? We are at a complete loss. However, as soon as we see the record for *Wiez*, we can easily determine that this is the title. For example:

Wiez.—Rok. 1 : nr. 1 (1958:luty)- .—Warzawa : RSW "Prasa-Ksiazka-Ruch," 1958-

Although we still have no idea what Wiez means, we can actually identify the components of the record:

The title is Wiez.
Rok. 1:nr. 1 (1958:luty)- refers to the enumeration of the serial.
It is published in Warzawa (Polish for Warsaw).
The publisher is RSW "Prasa-Ksiazka-Ruch."
It began publication in 1958 and is still published.

When cataloging serials, you may not always know the language in which the serial is written. However, with the establishment of cataloging standards, this is no longer as important as it used to be. You can search cataloging databases for a record and acquire the cataloging. Of course, you may not have subject headings attached to the imported record. Assigning subject headings takes some expertise with the language, but basic descriptive cataloging is now possible regardless of the language of the serial.

Subject Headings

Once we have prepared the descriptive portion of the catalog record, we may assign subject headings. Most people do not search for serials by subject, and yet there is good reason for applying standard headings. Many serials are not indexed in any periodical index. These serials may be inaccessible except through a subject search or staff recommendation. We still need to search through unindexed serials for articles of interest, but at least subject heading access through the catalog enables us to identify serials that pertain to our topic.

When assigning subject headings to any publication—serial or monograph—we examine the item to determine the subject. With serials, this is sometimes a very simple, straightforward procedure. In some cases, you need only examine the title as with *Ontario History, Russian Life*, or *Travel & Leisure*. Others titles are not so helpful, for example, *Inside Ireland* or *Connecting*. Both are travel magazines, but this is not evident from the titles.

You should examine the serial thoroughly. Examine more than one issue, if possible, since a single issue may be devoted to a specific topic. Many serials contain a statement of intent, which can help determine the subject coverage of a serial. Once the serial's coverage is determined, the next step is to choose the appropriate subject heading. Library of Congress subject headings are generally used, for example, *Europe—History* and *Genealogy—Ontario.*

Several common subdivisions reserved for serial publications are added at this point.

1. *—Periodicals:* This is the subdivision most commonly used with serials, for example, *Great Britain—History—Periodicals.* It indicates to the user that this item is a serial rather than a monograph. It is generally applied to all serials that are issued more or less regularly on an annual basis or more frequently. This means that if the serial is published twice a year, apply this subdivision. If the serial is published every second year, do not.

2. *—Congresses:* This subdivision is used for serial, as well as nonserial, proceedings of conferences, symposiums, workshops, congresses, and other meetings. If a serial covers the reports of an annual meeting, for example, then *—Congresses* should be applied. For example, *United States—History—Congresses* is assigned to a serial that reports on the annual meeting of the Association of American Historians.

3. *—Directories:* Most directories are considered to be serials. This subdivision, however, is given to all directories, whether they are serial publications or not. For example, *Canada—Industries—Directories* is assigned to a directory of industries in Canada, and *Hotels—Ireland—Directories* is assigned to a listing of Irish hotels.

4. *—Almanacs:* This subdivision is assigned to yearbooks and almanacs. A yearbook of folk music, for example, would be assigned the heading *Folk music—Almanacs.* If the serial is a general almanac that covers all topics, such as *Information Please Almanac,* very generic headings are assigned. They usually indicate only the country of publication, for example, *Almanacs, Canadian* or *Almanacs, American.* For Canadian almanacs, we have the option of indicating the language of the publication, for

example, *Almanacs, Canadian (English)* and *Almanacs, Canadian (French)*.

5. *—Bibliography:* Bibliographies are often encountered in serial form. These usually list all of the publications relevant to a specific topic for a particular year. For example, *British Archaeological Abstracts* contains references to articles and books that relate to British archaeology published during a specific year. In this case, the heading applied will be *Architecture—Bibliography*. Dealers' catalogs are another type of bibliography. They are bibliographies in that they list items on one specific topic, but they are also catalogs. They are generally given the subdivision combination—*Bibliography—Catalogues*, for example, *Art—Bibliography—Catalogues*.

6. *—Handbooks, manuals, etc.:* This subdivision is used for any handbook or manual.

7. *—Indexes:* This subdivision is used to designate indexes that are published in serial format. This includes most periodical and newspaper indexes such as *Humanities Index*. This subdivision is most often linked with periodicals such as *Humanities—Periodicals—Indexes* for *Humanities Index*.

8. *—Statistics:* This subdivision is used for any statistical publication. An example is the *Statistical Yearbook* from South Africa. The subject heading assigned to this publication would be *South Africa—Statistics*.

There are two other points of note.

1. For *Who's Who* publications, the standard subject heading is the name of the country with the addition of *—Biography—Directories*. *Brazil—Biography—Directories* is the heading assigned to *Who's Who in Brazil*. However, if the work focuses on a profession or other discernible group, use the subdivision *—Directories*. For example, *Who's Who in Philosophy* will be assigned the subject heading *Philosophers—Directories* and *Who's Who in Show Business* will have the subject heading *Entertainers—Directories*. Each of these works deals with one specific group of individuals.

2. Often the name of the serial's issuing body is used as a subject heading. This indicates that the journal provides information on the issuing society itself. The issuing body's name is often followed by the subdivision —*Periodicals*. For example, the *Archival Association of Atlantic Canada. Newsletter* is assigned the subject headings: *Archives—Maritime provinces—Periodicals* and *Archival Association of Atlantic Canada—Periodicals*.

When to Create a New Record

Knowing when to create a new catalog record for a serial is difficult. Two fundamental situations require the creation of a new serial record: the arrival of a new serial and a title change.

New Serial

The most obvious time to create a new record is when the library starts to receive a new serial. Usually the library staff waits until the serial arrives; however, many begin cataloging as soon as the order is placed. The order itself has been searched to verify ISSN, publisher, etc. Much of the information needed for the catalog record is at hand. Often a skeleton record will be put into the catalog consisting of basic title, publisher, and place of publication. In other cases, the complete record will be input. Either way, you must remember to note that the library has not yet received this serial. You can do this quite simply by recording *On Order* in the call number field of the record.

Title Change

Create a new record when a title changes. AACR2, rule 21.2C1 directs that a new entry must be made for a serial that undergoes a change in its title, whether or not the numeration is continuous. Rule 21.3B states that if the corporate body that sponsors or publishes the serial changes, a new record must be created. A change in the name of the corporate body usually indicates a shift in direction, emphasis, or makeup of the organization. Therefore, even if the serial title remains the same, its focus or perspective usually changes and the creation of a new catalog record is appropriate.

A link needs to be established between the old and new titles for the benefit of customers and staff. The old title is closed by recording the number of volumes in the physical description area and the last date of publication in the publication data area. A note is provided to link the old title to the new title. A link must also be made between the new title and the old title. The note added to the catalog record of the old title would be:

Continued by: Name of new title.

For the new title, the note would read:

Continues: Name of old title.

Other terms added as notes, as required, include:

Absorbed:
Absorbed by:
Formed by merger of:
Split to form:

Call Numbers

Call numbers are assigned, or not, according to library policy. They follow the same guidelines as applying call numbers to monographs.

Chapter 6

Processing and Shelving Arrangements

Objective: Upon successful completion of this chapter, the student will have demonstrated the ability to explain processing requirements and describe different approaches to organizing and shelving the serials collection.

During check in, the serials staff has on hand all the information needed to process the serial. For this reason, processing serials is usually done in conjunction with check in. The staff usually first notices problems during check in. Problems such as claiming, change of title, or even a change of publisher indicate that the serial could possibly need to be recataloged. If this is the case, set the journal aside for cataloging, or if there is a separate cataloging unit, forward the journal to cataloging.

Examine each issue carefully. Check to see if any pages are missing or if the issue has been damaged. If the issue is damaged in any way, contact the source of the serial—the agent or the publisher if you receive it direct—and request a new issue. If the issue is complete and in good condition, begin the processing.

1. Stamp the journal to indicate that it belongs to the library. It is recommended that the stamp be placed on the cover to make the issue instantly identifiable as the library's property. If the cover is glossy, apply a white label first and then stamp the label. If you do not use a label, the ink from the stamp can easily be wiped off. In some cases, you may need to apply a departmental or branch stamp as well. The purpose is to quickly identify where a particular issue should go. Location labels (e.g., open shelves) and/or call numbers may also need to be applied.

2. Stamp the date of receipt on the issue itself. This lets customers and staff know when the issue was received and allows you to project when the next issue should arrive.
3. Apply a security label if appropriate. Given the expense of security labels and the sheer volume of serial issues received, some libraries do not use security labels with serials.
4. Follow any special instructions noted in the check in, e.g., making a photocopy of specific title pages for certain individuals or routing the whole issue to certain people or departments. Routing slips usually can be generated by the automated system or a generic routing slip can be used.
5. Make a note for follow-up if it is time to weed or bind the serial.
6. Shelve the issues.

Figure 6.1 shows the elements that should be included in a **routing slip.**

There are many possible approaches to shelving the serials collection. The best approach for your individual library is the one that is best for your clientele since they are the people using the serials. Serials should be arranged for easy access, but an approach that is conve-

Serials routing slip	
Title: Journal of Modern History	
Location: [included for serials staff only—so they know where to place the journal once returned]	
Issue: [put in the issue information]	
Please cross off your name and send to the next person on the list. When all have seen the issue, please return it to the library.	
Name	Department
John Smith	IT
Manager, IT	IT

FIGURE 6.1. Sample Serials Routing Slip

nient for customers in a public library may not suit the needs of the academic library's clients.

SHELVING POLICIES

When establishing a shelving policy for serials, library staff must consider two basic issues: the overall approach to organizing the serials collection and "what is going where." All library managers face the question of what to do with their serials. Do we file them in a separate area or do we interfile them with the monographs? Do we use a combination of these two approaches? In many libraries, annuals are shelved with the monographs. For example, a Fodor's travel guide will be found with the monographs on travel. These serials are generally classified and, therefore, can be integrated with the main collection. The principal advantage to this approach is that items on the same subject are shelved together regardless of their format.

The treatment of periodicals is not as straightforward. Some library employees believe that *all* material on a subject should be brought together regardless of format. Employees of several smaller university libraries have taken the approach of interfiling annuals, periodicals, and monographs. This allows the user to find related material together in one section. However, this approach requires that serial publications be cataloged and classified.

Employees of other libraries have chosen a compromise. Annuals are shelved with the monographs, and periodicals are shelved in a separate area. This approach does not require that periodicals be classified. In fact, we do not even need to catalog them. This also allows us to house the periodical indexes in the same general area, enabling customers to use the indexes and the periodicals together. This approach also enables us to maintain greater control over the periodicals. Periodicals are subject to more vandalism than other library materials. Staff can more easily monitor the clientele using the collection if it is housed centrally. The main disadvantage to this approach is that monographs and serials on the same subject are housed separately. We lose the benefits of format integration. The advantages of the compromise approach (integrating annuals and separating periodicals) appear to outweigh the disadvantages, and most library managers have adopted this method of organizing the serials collection.

When we have determined the overall approach we will take to house the serials collection, we must decide how to organize the issues. There are three basic approaches: shelve all periodicals in alphabetical order based solely on the title; group periodicals by subject first and then shelve by title; or classify the serials. Classified serials could be filed in a separate serials area or interfiled with the monographs. Any decision is influenced by the organization of the library. If the library is subject divided, i.e., there are separate subject departments (social sciences, arts, etc.), the serials collection may be divided along the same lines. Social sciences serials will be housed in that department, arts serials in the arts area. Within each area, serials will be organized alphabetically by title. Even in a library that is not subject divided, periodicals can be organized initially by broad category: general periodicals (e.g., *Time, Newsweek*), science, social sciences, etc. Within each category, titles will be filed alphabetically. This type of subject division promotes browsing in subject areas of interest. This division, however, requires more work for staff. When the serial is first acquired, someone must decide in what area the serial will be shelved. This location is noted on the kardex and processing staff must stamp the location on issues as they arrive. A list of periodicals showing their locations must also be maintained. When customers request periodicals by title, we need to be able to direct them to the appropriate subject areas.

Another option is simply to shelve the periodicals in a single sequence, alphabetically by title. This requires that all periodicals be shelved in one area regardless of subject. This arrangement is easier for the staff. When shelving, we do not need to determine in which subject area a periodical belongs. We may have to worry about applying a subject location stamp during processing. However, this type of arrangement does not promote browsing by subject (i.e., you cannot find all of the history periodicals in one spot). To compensate for this, some library personnel produce user guides that list the periodicals that pertain to a particular topic. With this list in hand, the customers can still browse the shelves to a certain extent.

The third option is to classify the serials and shelve them with the monograph collection. This would bring all material on the same topic together into one area. However, since so many serials are interdisciplinary, the call number assigned could prove not to be that useful.

The size of serials can pose problems for shelving when the collection is integrated. Many libraries have a separate folio section since folios cannot be shelved with the main run of the collection. The same folio section is generally used to accommodate periodicals. If you do have a folio section, signage is needed to direct customers to that section. The section itself must be clearly marked. Some libraries use book dummies that direct the customer from where periodicals should be found to the folio section where they are actually shelved.

The format of a serial can also pose a problem. If a title is in more than one format (e.g., back issues on microfilm and current issues in paper copy), signage is needed that will direct the customer from one format to the other. Book dummies with appropriate instructions are adequate. In the case described, the instructions on the dummy might state: All issues before the current year are found on microfilm. See the microfilm section.

"What Goes Where"

Most libraries are not large enough to house all their serials on the open shelves. Therefore, we must examine the serials collection and the physical constraints and decide what should go where. In most libraries, serials (annuals or less frequent publications) and periodicals (items published more frequently than once a year) are treated differently. Serials are usually shelved with the monographs; periodicals are usually shelved separately in a periodicals area. The question remains: How many issues will be kept on the open shelves? For example, for a serial that the library keeps permanently, the current issue only may go on the open shelves. Earlier issues may be found in a closed stacks area. Alternatively, you may keep the current ten years on the open shelves and earlier ones in the stacks. For periodicals, you may want to keep only the current year on the open shelves and shelve all others in the stacks. The size of the collection, the physical constraints imposed by the library, and the needs of the user group determine the library's policy of what goes where.

Certain generalizations can be made with regard to what goes where:

1. Current issues of a serial or periodical should go on the open shelves. In most cases, people want to see these issues. Any other arrangement would place too heavy a demand on retrieval staff. In certain exceptions, library managers might decide to keep rare, valuable, or controversial items in a controlled area.
2. Bibliographies should always be on the open shelves. Customers need access to all issues of a bibliography. If they are not shelved in the open access area, they are not used.

Whatever policy the library adopts should be applied consistently for the benefit of customers and staff. If, for example, the library policy is to keep the current five years on the open shelves, all departments should adhere to this system if at all possible. The policy must also be communicated to customers. They need to know that the library keeps only the current issues on the open shelves. They also need to know what to do if they want access to earlier issues. Signage is important in conveying this message.

TYPES OF SHELVING

Many libraries use display shelves to house their current issues. These shelves tilt at an angle with a ridge running along the bottom to hold the periodical in place. The current issues can be placed flat on the shelf with the cover in full view. Titles are easy to find and the display promotes public awareness of the periodical collection. However, only the current issue can be stored in this manner. Customers need to know where earlier issues can be found. Even if you store the earlier issues under the display shelf (most display shelves lift up so that earlier issues can be stacked on the shelf underneath), many customers will not know where to look. Appropriate signage is needed, e.g., a notice that says: Lift the shelf for earlier issues.

HOW TO SHELVE

Follow basic guidelines when shelving periodicals and serials.

1. Periodicals are usually thin and flimsy (think of a copy of *Time*) and need support on the shelves. A periodical box will offer this support. However, leave enough room between the top of the box and the shelf above. When customers remove issues from the box, they tend to pull the issues—not the box—up and out. If there is not enough room between the shelf above and the box itself, issues will be damaged. Metal periodical boxes that have an open front allow the customers to pull the issues straight out; this reduces wear and tear on the issues.
2. If boxes are used, a decision must be made regarding how the periodicals in each box will be organized. Should the current issue go at the front of the box (right side as the box sits on the shelf) or at the back (left side)? Note that the spine of the serial faces out toward the shelver/customer. Once this decision is made, it should be followed consistently.

Both approaches offer advantages. Arranging the issues in the box with the later issues at the back (left side of the box) is easier for binding purposes. When binding, the issues go in chronological order from the earliest to the latest (i.e., January, then February, then March, etc.). When this practice is followed for individual issues, customers become familiar with this order and adapt to use of bound volumes easily. If the box is organized with the latest issue at the front (right-hand side of the box), the cover of the current issue is visible. However, this arrangement requires reversing the order of the issues for binding.

As current issues are shelved, older issues may need to be weeded or moved to another location. If, for example, display shelving is used, as the current issue is shelved the next most current issue will need to be moved to the shelf underneath the display shelf. This in turn may trigger the relocation of the oldest issue in the stack under the display shelf to a closed stacks area. Shelving serials is often a multistep process.

Shelving serials may seem to be a straightforward operation. A series of policies and procedures need to be in place, however, for this simple practice to function efficiently.

Chapter 7

Claims

Objective: Upon successful completion of this chapter, the student will have demonstrated the ability to issue claims.

REASONS FOR PLACING CLAIMS

A **claim** is a notification to the supplier of the serial that there is a problem. A claim is generated in the following situations:

1. *Defective issues:* If the issue the library receives is defective or damaged in any way claim a replacement issue from the supplier. Clearly indicate that the claim is for a *replacement* copy. The supplier needs to know that a problem exists somewhere in the distribution process that must be resolved. Also check with the supplier on how to handle defective issues. Some suppliers require that the defective issue be returned. Others simply take our word for the problem and we can discard the issue.
2. *Nonreceipt of issues:* This is the most common reason for a claim. In some cases, as you check in an issue, you notice that an earlier issue has not been received. In other cases, a customer may alert you to the nonreceipt of a particular issue. Sometimes an issue may have been lost in the mail. Alternatively, nonreceipt can mean that the serial has stopped coming. Perhaps you failed to renew your subscription, or perhaps your name was inadvertently left off the mailing list. A claim will help identify the reason why you have stopped receiving the serial.

PLACING CLAIMS

An automated system issues claims automatically. When you first enter information concerning a serial into the system, you will be asked to establish a pattern of receipt. For example, issues arrive in March, May, July, and October. When the March issue comes, the system "expects" an issue to arrive. If it does not, the system automatically generates a claim. In some cases, the library's computer "talks" directly with the supplier's computer and sends the claim electronically. Otherwise, a paper claim form is printed that the serials staff can fax or mail.

In a manual system, claiming is usually done when you check in an issue. You note that the previous issue has not been received, and you fill in a claim form. Client requests are also helpful in identifying claims. A client asks for a certain issue, and upon checking the kardex, you discover that the issue has not been checked in. A claim is then sent.

Identifying serials that have simply stopped coming in is more difficult. If you are not checking in an issue of the serial, the fact that issues have not been received may not be noticed. The kardex should be thoroughly examined at least twice a year to identify serials that have stopped arriving.

An automated system generates its own claim forms. For manual claims, a standard form is useful.

Examples of Automated Claim Forms

Figures 7.1 and 7.2 are two examples of automated claim forms. They are generic in that they can be used for any serial (and for some monographs also). They are also succinct. The cardinal rule is to let the supplier know that an issue is missing and to do so clearly and concisely (while remaining civil).

Manual Form

Figure 7.3 is an example of a manual claim form. This form can be used for any claim. Fill in the boxes with the appropriate information. The form also allows the supplier to record his or her information/response before returning the form to you.

Vendor's name: Your name:
Vendor's address: Your library's address:

Date: SUBSCRIPTION CLAIM
Re: Our subscription to: **Title of serial to claim**
               Year   Volume   Issue
We have not yet received: **List issues not received here**

Remarks: **This used to explain any problems. If this is a second or third claim, it should be noted here.**

Our order number is:

Charge or invoice number:

Your immediate attention to this matter is appreciated.

FIGURE 7.1. Sample of Automated Claim Form

Whenever you claim an issue, a record of the claim should be kept. An automated system may record the claim on a claim screen (a separate section of the serials function that shows all the claims made for a particular serial). In a manual system, you should note on the kardex that an issue has been claimed and keep a photocopy of the actual claim. Allow a reasonable time for the supplier to respond. A "reasonable time" is hard to define. Obviously a claim sent to Great Britain will take longer to elicit a response than a claim sent within your community. Within North America, we generally allow four to six weeks. For all other countries, allow six to eight weeks. If the claim has not been resolved after a suitable period of time, send another claim notice. Mark this as a second (or third) notice to emphasize to the supplier that this matter deserves attention. It is important to allow the supplier time to respond to the claim.

If a second or third claim is not successful, write a firm but polite letter explaining the problem and highlighting the need for the issue.

CLAIM 1

Date of claim:

To: **Vendor's address**

Title: **Title of serial to claim**
Publisher: **Put in to ensure that you are claiming the right serial**
ISSN:
Year/Volume claimed:
Quantity claimed:

Our order number:
Customer number:

Ship claimed pieces   **Your address**
or reply to:

Supplier: check appropriate response(s):
Claimed item sent on _____
Not yet published. Due
Back ordered. Due
Out of print.
Not our title.
No record of this order.

Remarks:

FIGURE 7.2. Sample of Automated Claim Form

A record must be kept of this correspondence. Many library managers cancel serials subscriptions when they have had problems with claims.

WHEN TO CLAIM

Generally, a claim should be sent four to six weeks after the date the serial issue was expected. This allows for mailing time. Some libraries wait six months before claiming. Such a long delay could cause problems as some publishers do not keep back issues of a serial. By the time your claim reaches the publisher, the issue may be out of print. A reclaim (second claim) is generally sent six to eight weeks after the first claim.

It is important to become familiar with the supplier's policies and practices as some do not keep any back issues. If this is the case, a

LIBRARY NAME
ADDRESS
CITY, STATE, POSTAL CODE

TITLE: _____ Vol.   No.   Issue date:
TO: ☐ 1st Notice
                                         ☐ 2nd Notice

FROM: Contact person's name,
        Library Name,
        Address,
        City, State
        Postal Code

Our request or other communication concerning the item named above is shown in our message below. Please answer by checking your reply or by explaining under "Remarks." Return this form and requested material, if any, to the name indicated above.

OUR MESSAGE	YOUR MESSAGE
☐ Listed issues have not been received	☐ Item sent on
☐ Last issue received	☐ Item not yet published
☐ Send invoice for	☐ Never published
☐ Payment has been sent	☐ Cannot find your order
☐ We are receiving duplicate issues	☐ Ceased publication
Remarks:	Remarks:

FIGURE 7.3. Sample Manual Claim Form

claim must be issued as soon as possible. Claims for dailies such as newspapers are usually issued immediately.

Most suppliers will not handle claims for issues that are a year old. In the case of lapsed serials, the supplier can usually supply the current issues, but any others must be ordered as a backset.

Chapter 8

Binding

Objective: Upon successful completion of this chapter, the student will have demonstrated the ability to explain the purpose of binding and to identify the steps in preparing serials for binding.

Binding is an integral part of the activities of most serial departments. Binding is done in order to preserve investment in a journal. Serials left loose on the shelves tend to get ripped, stolen, or quickly lost. A bound volume is sturdier than a single issue and more difficult to steal or misplace. Furthermore, shelving is more straightforward since it is much easier to shelve one bound volume than five or six individual issues. Binding not only preserves the serial but also makes it easier for customers to locate needed issues. Most library employees recognize the importance of binding and bind their serials on a regular basis. If a library does not plan to retain a title, it may not be cost effective to bind that serial. Managers of small libraries who choose to keep only the current few years may decide not to bind their serials.

Most library employees do not do the binding themselves. Instead, they have a contract with a commercial binder. The binding operation usually takes three to four weeks. This is an inconvenience, but given the cost of setting up an in house binding unit, most library managers accept the inconvenience for the sake of preserving the serial. Rush binding is usually available at additional cost.

FACTORS TO CONSIDER BEFORE BINDING

Preparing the journals for binding is a very time-consuming and labor intensive job that requires several steps.

1. *Identify the journals to be bound:* Any journal that the library plans to retain should be bound to preserve it. If a journal is not to be kept, it would be a waste of time and money to bind the issues.

2. *When to bind:* Binding generally occurs when a complete volume is received. There would be no logic in binding a journal when only the first three issues of a quarterly have arrived. However, in some cases, we may want to bind more frequently. Two factors should be considered: the frequency of publication and the size of the issues. A monthly publication will generally require more frequent binding than an annual. A serial containing 200 to 300 pages per issue will be bound more frequently than a serial with ten to twelve pages per issue.

   Avoid having a bound volume that exceeds three inches in width. Two inches is the optimum width. Therefore, examine the issues to determine how and when to bind them. We may decide to bind January-June and then July-December or January-March, April-June, July-September, and October-December. Once the binding pattern is established, follow it consistently whenever possible. So, if we bind January-June, July-December for 1994, then we should do the same for 1995, 1996, etc. This binding information should be recorded somewhere, preferably in the check-in system. This means, for example, that as you check in the June issue, you see that you now have a complete set for binding.

3. *When to send to binding:* Some managers of libraries like to bind as soon as possible. This lessens the possibility that issues will be lost or damaged. Generally, we like to leave at least one issue on the shelves to let the customers know that we still have a subscription to the serial. Therefore, we tend to wait until one more issue is received. For example, if we bind annually, we wait until the first issue of the next volume is received before we bind. If we bind January-June, we wait until the July issue is received. Others wait for their "quiet" period (generally the summer) to bind. Use whatever approach works best.

   The library may need to wait until it acquires missing or damaged issues. However, after an established number of claim notices (usually two), the volume should be bound to avoid further loss. In this case, the spine of the bound volume should be marked "Incomplete."

4. *How to bind:* All serials used to be bound in the best binding available. This is no longer possible. The best binding (generally called **class A binding** with full buckram, sewn binding, and rounded and backed spine) is also the most expensive. When a library is binding thousands of volumes per year, the expense can be considerable. In an effort to cut down on costs, binders are experimenting with other types of binding. The most common are:

- **monoetching** (instead of being sewn, the issues are glued);
- **econobinding** (lamination of the original covers); and
- **econo-plus binding** (original covers are scanned, reproduced, and laminated).

Binding is determined by library policy. Generally, the following guidelines are used:

- If the serial is heavily used and if the library intends to retain it permanently, use the class A binding.
- If the serial is not so heavily used, but the library intends to retain it permanently, use monoetching.
- If the serial is not heavily used and the library only intends to keep the issues for five years or less, use econobinding.
- If the serial is not heavily used and the library wants to retain the issues for between five and ten years, use the econo-plus binding.

5. *Indexes:* Many journal publishers create their own indexes to a volume. Obviously this index cannot be printed until the volume is complete. If the index is to be bound with the volume, binding cannot be done until the index is received.

PREPARING FOR BINDING

Once we have identified the journals to be bound, we prepare them for binding.

1. *Collect the journals:* Some library employees leave markers or dummies in place of the journals to let customers know that the issues have gone to binding.
2. *Collate the issues:* Some binders will **collate** the issues for an extra cost. Other binders, however, will simply bind the issues as they are received. To be on the safe side, put the issues in chronological order with the oldest on top and the most current on the bottom.
3. *Fasten the issues together:* Some library employees tie the issues together with string. Others use plastic bags. Plastic bags can be retrieved from the binder and reused.
4. *Fill in the binding slip:* Most commercial binders have a standard binding form. You simply fill in the boxes or blanks. Several decisions need to be made at this time.

   - *Binding title:* Serials often have very long titles. It is often impossible to print the whole name on the spine. Use an abbreviated *binding title* instead. Use the abbreviation that will be understood by the public. Let common sense be the guide. For example, abbreviate "historical" to "hist." rather than "histori." Avoid words that might offend. For example, do not abbreviate "association" to "ass." Use "assoc." instead.
   - *Information to be found on spine:* The title is an obvious choice to be printed on the spine. Include volume, issue, part, and date. This helps the customer to identify the actual contents of the bound volume. Also, note the call number if applicable.
   - *Covers:* It is a good idea to leave the covers on the issues because it is easier to identify the actual issues by looking for the covers. The only exception is when enumeration of the pages is continuous (i.e., issue no. 1 ends with p. 256 and issue no. 2 begins with p. 257). In these serials, the text is usually continuous as well. Having covers bound in here would be confusing.
   - *Advertisements:* Some serials have pages of advertisements at the end of the issue. These do not contribute to the content of the serial, so some library employees remove them.
   - *Table of contents and indexes:* These are used to help identify where to find a certain article. Some library employees leave

them with the issue with which they were received. Others remove them from individual issues and group them together. Generally, tables of contents will be bound together in the front of the volume and indexes are bound at the end.

- *Special instructions:* If a map or fold-out supplement is included, a pocket may be needed. If the volume needs special treatment, note it on the binding slip.
- *Type of binding:* Most libraries prefer sewn binding because it is more durable. It is, however, the most expensive binding. An alternative may be to have the serial glued (called mono-etching). For important serials or those that are heavily used, a sewn binding is recommended. If cost is a factor, gluing is possible for serials that are not heavily used. See the discussion of binding types earlier in this chapter.
- *Trim or not:* Binders have stock sizes of binding. The binding is done by a computer that works with preset sizes. The binder selects the size that is closest to the actual size of the issues. This may mean that the serial must be trimmed and then text could be lost. If you do not want trimming, indicate "Do not trim." This may cost more, but it guarantees the integrity of the issues.
- *Color of binding and spine label:* How important is the color of the binding? It would be easy to bind everything in green or red. However, color could be extremely useful. Some libraries use color to indicate subject. History journals appear in red, travel in green, literature in blue, etc. Customers can now browse the shelves and identify journals of interest simply by looking for the appropriate color. Color can also be used to indicate binding pattern: bind all the red journals in February; green in March, etc. This is not useful for the public but could be invaluable for the staff. The color of the writing on the binding must also be considered. Generally, white or black is used. Use white on a dark cover and black on a light cover.

All of this information must be included on the binding slip. Once the information for the binding slip has been finalized, record it somewhere so that next time this serial is bound, the data will be available.

Each time you send issues of a journal for binding, you want the volume to be bound in the same fashion as previous volumes. This also applies to the position of the lettering on the spine. You want all issues to be the same so that you can easily run your eye along the spines when looking for a particular issue. For this reason, a **rub** is often sent with the binding. A rub is generally a photocopy of the spine of a bound volume. When making the copy, put a pencil or pen at the top and bottom of the spine to show where the spine ends and begins. This helps the binder determine where each facet (e.g., title, volume, etc.) of the spine label should go.

Most binders have automated systems. When you send a serial to be bound the first time, you make all the decisions discussed earlier. All these instructions are recorded in the binder's computer and a title number is assigned to the journal. When preparing the next set of issues for binding, you need specify only the title number. However, if the binding requirements for a particular set of issues differ in any way from the usual manner in which the serial is bound, this must be noted. Perhaps this time the serial has a supplement. This fact must be noted on the spine. Perhaps the serial is incomplete. This must also be noted. If the variation represents a permanent change (e.g., the serial has changed size or frequency), it must be described as such. Otherwise, the binder will bind the issues with the exception noted, but will not change the binding record.

A record should be kept of the issues that have gone to binding. Most binders use a three-part form and one copy is retained by the sender. This should be stored in a convenient spot in case a customer requests an issue of a serial that cannot be found. Staff members need access to a list of serials that have gone to binding and when they have gone, so that they can inform the public. When the binding order returns, check it thoroughly. Make sure the issues are bound in proper order. Check the spine label to ensure that the information is accurate and complete.

Chapter 9

Renewals

Objective: Upon successful completion of this chapter, the student will have demonstrated the ability to renew subscriptions.

Renewing a subscription would seem to be a simple operation: the publisher sends a notice that a subscription is about to lapse and asks for permission to renew the subscription, or the publisher simply requests payment for a new subscription. Unfortunately, the process is not nearly as straightforward as it would appear. Many publishers or agents send a renewal notice well in advance of the end of the subscription. This is done to ensure the continued receipt of the serial. Good suppliers will send renewal notices and then allow time to respond before sending the second or third renewal notice. They will also mark the notice: 1st notice, 2nd notice, etc.

Unfortunately, this does not always happen. Some suppliers seem to send a new batch of renewal notices on a weekly basis. You, of course, begin to worry that the renewal you have already submitted has not been received. You may be tempted to respond to one of these renewal notices and then end up with two subscriptions to the same serial. Check with the supplier first before you send a second payment for a renewal. Some suppliers, especially small publishers, do not send out renewal notices. They rely upon you to contact them to renew your subscription.

RENEWAL TERMINOLOGY

Several terms relating to renewals need clarification.

Invoice: An **invoice** is a request for payment when the actual volume or issue has already been received by the library. Generally, the invoice accompanies the material. The invoice should clearly state: "Please pay this amount." Invoices are also called **debit memos** or DMs.

Proforma invoice: This is also a request for payment. However, unlike the invoice, the **proforma invoice** demands payment before the item is shipped. The supplier will send the item only upon receipt of payment.

Renewal list: A **renewal list** itemizes titles that are currently being sent to you by the supplier. You review the list and either approve or cancel the titles. You return the list to the supplier. This is not an invoice. No payment is required. It is only the preliminary step in determining the amount you owe for renewals.

Renewal invoice: Based on the approved/canceled titles on the renewal list, the agent will issue a **renewal invoice.** Treat this as you would an invoice.

Credit: Also called a credit memo or CM, a **credit** is issued if the supplier owes you money. This is often the result of a cancelation (when you had already prepaid the subscription) or a currency fluctuation. When you paid the agent's invoice, the pound might have been worth $1.30, so you paid CD$13.00 for a £10 serial. Now, as the agent prepares to pay the actual vendor, the pound is worth $1.15. The agent needs to pay only $11.50. You paid the agent $13.00 so he or she issues you a credit for $1.50. These memos are used against an invoice from the same supplier. You then pay only the difference owing.

Supplementary invoice: The **supplementary invoice** generally comes only from agents. The agents estimate the cost of the renewal. However, since they have not been invoiced for the actual titles, they can supply you with an estimated cost only. You then can, if you wish, receive a supplementary invoice that indicates the firm price. In some cases, you would need to pay the difference (if any) upon receipt of the supplementary invoice. In other cases, you would wait until the next invoice to pay the difference. If payment is required upon receipt of the supplementary invoice, this is usually clearly indicated.

Statement: A **statement** is a summary of all of the invoices and credits that you have with a supplier. It is *not* an invoice and does not require payment. It is only to let you know where the account stands at present.

HANDLING RENEWALS

A serial may be renewed in several different ways depending upon how the library receives it.

By an Agent

If you receive a serial through an agent, that agent will handle all the renewals. Do *not* make any renewals with the publisher directly. If the library previously received a serial directly from the publisher, but now goes through an agent, the original supplier will often keep sending renewals to the library. He or she does not know that the library now receives the serial through an agent and is concerned that you have canceled your subscription. In such cases, excellent documentation and record keeping on your part are vital. You need to know from whom you receive a serial. Any concerns or renewals must be addressed to that source only. If you keep receiving renewal notices, contact your agent who, hopefully, will deal with the supplier.

Agents will usually invoice you once or twice a year. They "package" all the serials that you receive in one list and send this renewal list to you. You review the list and note any serials that you wish to cancel. You are then invoiced based on the results of the renewal list. Agents also invoice you in one currency. If you renew on your own, you must deal with many different currencies.

The advantages of using agents are obvious when it comes to renewals. They bill you once or twice a year in one common currency. They will also, if you wish, continue to renew a serial until you notify them to stop. They usually notify you if an increase in cost exceeds a percentage already agreed upon (e.g., more than 10 percent). Otherwise, the serial is automatically renewed.

There are also disadvantages; agents tend to renew your subscription and prepay even before they bill you. For example, the subscription for serial "Y" comes up for renewal in January. The agent renews the subscription and pays for it out of his or her funds. The library is then billed for this serial in July. If you wish to cancel this serial, you cannot do so immediately. You have already prepaid the serial until December. The earliest that you can cancel it is December.

Once you receive the invoice or list of serials that are being renewed, review the list thoroughly. Ensure that each title is accurate and that you are being billed for the edition or format that you want. Check to make sure that you are receiving the number of copies that you want. Also make sure that any credits that the agent has issued have been applied.

Direct Renewals

Direct renewals are for serials that the library receives directly from the publisher. The great advantage to a direct renewal is that you have complete control over the subscription; it is renewed or canceled at your convenience. The following list discusses disadvantages to ordering directly.

- Invoices are received throughout the year. In contrast to using an agent, in which case you are billed once or twice a year, you must handle renewals throughout the year when dealing directly.
- The volume of subscriptions can be a problem. With an agent, you deal with one or perhaps two companies. When ordering directly, you are dealing with many suppliers. Often, you will only receive one serial from a supplier. In other cases, you receive two or more serials from the same supplier. Accurate records must be maintained to ensure that each title has been renewed and paid for, and that you are paying the right supplier.
- Some smaller publishers do not send renewals. They rely on you to renew the titles. You must keep records of these titles.
- You must keep accurate records of the whereabouts of the publisher. If you do not receive a renewal notice, you need to contact the publisher. The hunt for a current address can often be time consuming and frustrating.
- You must deal in many different currencies. The bill must be paid in the currency demanded by the publisher. You could be paying in British pounds, French francs, U.S. dollars, etc. Accu-

rate records are necessary and exchange rates must be monitored.
- You must keep records of all communications relating to each serial.

Whether you receive a serial from an agent or from the publisher, the renewal needs to be paid. The serials staff will usually verify that the invoice is accurate, that any credits have been applied to the invoice, that the subscription is actually wanted, and then arrange for payment. The fund account number needs to recorded on the invoice to ensure that the funds are deducted from the correct account. Payment could be handled through a central financial services department or through the serials unit itself.

This is not the end of the record keeping. Each invoice, whether direct or from an agent, must be linked to an account and to the actual check that pays the invoice. If problems arise later, you must be able to refer immediately to the actual check. Make note of the titles that are being renewed, when the check was issued for each title, and when the renewal subscription will expire. This information can usually be recorded on the kardex or in the serial's record in an automated system. You will also need to keep the balance in the accounts up to date. Given the ever-increasing cost of serials, being able to determine the balance left in the serials budget is imperative. Cancelations are often made based on this balance. Accurate record keeping is extremely important.

Chapter 10

Cessations

Objective: Upon successful completion of this chapter, the student will have demonstrated the ability to describe how library employees handle cessations.

Cessations are titles that have ceased publication. For whatever reason, the publisher will no longer produce the title. Sometimes, the publisher will send you notice that he or she intends to stop publishing a title. Often your agent will inform you. You may find out that a title has ceased when you try to claim some issues.

With cessations, a number of items must be addressed:

1. Make sure that any credit for a prepaid subscription is received. Unfortunately, if the publisher goes bankrupt, this may not be possible. Otherwise, publishers usually issue a credit.
2. Notify financial services or whoever pays the invoice. This will ensure that no further payments are issued for the ceased serial.
3. Notify cataloging. The cessation of a title should be recorded in the catalog record.
4. Clean up any other records. Note the cessation in the kardex or stock cards. Change any records in a union list to indicate the serial has ceased.

TITLE CHANGES

One special type of cessation is a title change. It is the cessation of one title and the beginning of another. We discussed title changes and cataloging earlier. However, several problems caused by title changes still need to be addressed.

1. The purchase order for the new title may not be the same. If a different purchase order number is listed, record this. Later, when you receive an invoice for the new title, you will be able to identify the actual title.
2. Invoices can be confusing. You could receive an invoice for the old title (for the issues received) and a separate invoice for the new title, or you could receive one invoice for the two titles. Whatever the case, check these invoices carefully. Make sure that you are not paying twice for the same issues.
3. There can be problems with renewal lists. Agents are generally very good when dealing with title changes. However, make sure that the title change has been noted on the renewal list. One library employee reports having paid for the same title twice (once under the old title and once under the new) for five years before the agent cleared up the problem!

CANCELLATIONS

A cancellation is a notification that the library will no longer be receiving a serial. Most often the library does the canceling, but an agent could also cancel a title. If the agent has lost the rights to handle a certain title, he or she will cancel your subscription to the title. You are then free to try to obtain this serial through other means. There are several reasons for canceling a serial:

- *Cost:* The cost of the serial may have increased by 50 or even 100 percent. With a limited budget, the library may no longer be able to afford this serial.
- *No longer appropriate to the collection:* Every library has a collection policy—a statement of what it intends to collect. Serials undergo changes. The focus of a serial may have changed so that it is no longer appropriate for the library's collection.
- *Poor service:* If you have more claims than you have actual issues or if you spend too much time claiming a serial, it may not be worthwhile continuing the subscription. You are not providing good service to your customers if your collection has large or frequent gaps.
- *You may now be receiving the serial through other means:* If you want to start receiving the serial through an agent instead of di-

rectly, you will cancel the serial. You might begin to receive the serial as a donation, in which case you will cancel your subscription.

- *Budgetary constraints:* In some cases, because of the ever-increasing costs of serials, you may have to cut back on the number of titles you receive. This type of cancellation must be done very carefully. Conduct a thorough collection evaluation to determine the impact of canceling each title before making your decision.
- *Resource sharing:* One response to budgetary problems is to share resources. Managers of two or more libraries may decide to share their serial titles. Instead of each subscribing to the same title, only one library will continue a subscription and will make that title available to customers of the other libraries. This type of sharing will work only if all libraries continue to participate in the cooperative agreement.
- *Available in a different format:* In some cases, the library may decide to cancel a subscription in one format and restart the subscription in a different format.

If the library staff decides to cancel a serial, several steps must be taken:

1. You must notify the supplier of your decision to cancel a serial. Make sure that the request for cancellation is clear. Also state when the cancellation should begin (i.e., immediately, at the end of the current subscription, with vol. 24, etc.).
2. Notify the financial services department or whoever pays the invoices. This will ensure that they do not pay any renewals that may slip through.
3. Notify reference staff; they provide reference service with serials and need to know what is to be canceled and when.
4. Note this information in any records, such as the kardex or automated check-in system. Note that the title is canceled and when the cancellation is to take effect.
5. Keep a copy of any correspondence you have with the supplier. Later, if you find that you are still receiving the serial, you will need to refer to your own records.
6. Clean up any other records such as union lists that need to be changed.

Chapter 11

Automation

Objective: Upon successful completion of this chapter, the student will have demonstrated the ability to describe the role of automation in serials management.

More and more library personnel are examining the automation of serials functions. So far, we have discussed the effect of automation upon each serial function individually. However, we need to bring these individual discussions together for an overall view of the major advantages and disadvantages of an automated system.

ADVANTAGES OF AUTOMATION

- *Prediction patterns:* Based on the past pattern of receipt (i.e., when issues arrive), the system can "predict" when the next issue should appear. This also helps in reference work. You can give customers an estimated time of arrival for a particular issue.
- *Check in:* Check in is done online. This allows everyone who has access to the system to view the holdings. Also, the sum of the check-in screens gives you a list of actual issues received.
- *Claiming:* Claiming can be done automatically based on the predicted date of receipt.
- *Routing list:* Routing lists can be produced automatically. You input people's names or positions (i.e., Children's Librarian) of those who are to receive the serial, and the system will generate the list.
- *Binding schedule:* A binding schedule can be established based on past practice. When you check in an issue, the system checks the binding function and determines if it is time to bind. If so, a reminder is printed or sent to you electronically.

- *Cataloging:* Cataloging can be done online, so everyone with access can view the information found in a catalog record.
- *Physical preparation:* The system can generate spine labels automatically upon check in.
- *Payment:* Payment schedules can be determined. Based upon the date a subscription is renewed (which you input), the system can alert you when a subscription is about to expire.
- *Source of receipt:* Source of the serial, from an agent (and which one), direct, or through gifts and exchanges can be noted.
- *Bar codes:* Bar codes can be printed to allow circulation.
- *Circulation:* Circulation and related functions can be handled through an automated system.
- *Article delivery:* Many automated systems can be linked with a vendor's system. The request for a copy of an article can be done through the system.
- *Union lists:* Union lists are easily produced. In a multibranch system the sum of all of the serials and their holdings is the union list. Often these can be downloaded into a word processing package and then printed.
- *Customer access:* Customers can access information about a serial through the check-in screen, holdings screen, cataloging screen, etc.
- *Report production:* Reports can be produced on a wide variety of topics.
- *Location:* In an automated system all serials functions are in one place. There is no need to keep the variety of files required in a manual system.

DISADVANTAGES OF AUTOMATION

1. An automated system is expensive. It also requires extensive training and, in fact, the staff who use the system become "expert staff." Almost anyone can figure out how to check in using a kardex. Only trained staff can do check in using an automated system. This means that other staff cannot assist when needed.
2. Setting up the system is very time consuming since all the information has to be recorded in MARC record format. When you start up the new automated system, a great deal of staff time must be invested to provide the system with the information it

needs. For each serial we must input the prediction pattern, binding schedules, routing lists, etc. The functions in a serials system take a great deal of memory and storage space. A powerful computer is required.

Chapter 12

New Technology

Objective: Upon successful completion of this chapter, the student will have demonstrated the ability to describe the impact of new technology on serials.

During the past few years, new technologies have had a major impact on libraries and on library serial collections in particular.

- *Serials on CD-ROM:* Several years of a serial may be stored on one CD-ROM. Given the space shortages that most libraries face, CD-ROMs offer a means to acquire the serial without the bulk. CD-ROMs also allow enhanced search capabilities such as searching for key words in the text of articles.
- *Serials on diskette:* Diskettes provide the same benefits as CD-ROMs. Diskettes also allow the customers to manipulate data for their own purposes.
- *Electronic serials:* Some serials exist only in electronic form. An online serial is available to readers as soon as it is written, so the articles are much more up to date than articles in paper serials. Medical and science journals are perfect candidates for electronic delivery since people in these fields want the *most* current information. Many almanacs and yearbooks also benefit from electronic availability.
- *Video:* Very few serials are distributed on videotape, but several travel magazines have started to issue supplements on video. These videos offer sounds and scenes to entice the traveler.

The new technologies have definitely benefited serials. However, the new technologies are not without problems.

ARCHIVING

Electronic serials are also difficult to archive unless the body issuing the serial does its own archiving. Often only the most current copy or last few copies of the serial are available. Customers and staff basically have no immediate access to older issues of the serial.

Unfortunately, no easy solutions are offered for these problems. Staff at many libraries provide access to the current serial through CD-ROM or an online service, and provide access to the older issues by purchasing microfiche or microfilm copies of the serial. Others provide a document delivery system whereby customers can request articles from older issues and the library will obtain them from elsewhere.

STORAGE

Storage is a major problem, especially if a serial comprises different formats (e.g., print, but with video supplements and older issues on microfiche). Collections are usually arranged by format. Books and other paper copies are kept in one location, microforms in another, CD-ROMs in another, and videos usually with other audiovisual formats. A means of linking all of these formats and locations is needed. If every single edition of the journal has the same formats, a single note can be made in the catalog record stating: "Fiche at _____; paper copy at _____." What do you do when only a few issues have fiche or video supplements? Can you imagine the notes!

v. 3, no. 4 has video at _____; fiche at _____
v. 3, no. 5 has fiche at _____
v. 4, no. 1 has film at _____; video at _____

You also need to put a linking note or instruction on the serial itself to guide the customer.

EQUIPMENT

The equipment needed to accommodate new technologies can be daunting. Film/fiche requires readers, storage equipment, and printers. Discs require storage equipment, computers, and printers. Also, some discs are only compatible with certain systems (i.e., Mac, etc). For online journals, computer equipment is needed, perhaps modems or an Internet connection, and printers. Videotape requires video equipment.

CHECK-IN

How do you check in an issue that has various components or supplements that are found in different locations? In theory, each format requires a separate check-in screen, so there would be one for fiche, one for paper copies, etc. For a serial that regularly has different formats, we could produce the appropriate check-in screens. We can also produce a prediction pattern. A serial that occasionally produces a video or a fiche supplement poses problems. How can you predict a date of arrival for each format when each is published irregularly? How do you check in an online journal? Do you check it in? At present, there are no good answers to these questions.

ACCESS

Customers need to know where to find a journal and all its parts. How do we facilitate this when the journal is in many formats? Signage that links the various components of the serial is very important. Signage is also required to direct the customer to the location housing each format.

Technology will continue to exert a major influence on our profession. It progresses so quickly that we can barely keep up with what is new let alone find satisfactory solutions to the challenges presented by technical developments of the past few years. We need to be innovative, flexible, and generous in sharing our knowledge and expertise with one another if we are going to take control of new technologies and use them to serve the needs of our customers.

Glossary

AACR2: *Anglo-American Cataloguing Rules,* Second Edition, 2002 revision (Chicago: American Library Association). This is the basic work that establishes standard cataloging practices.

access point: A name or term through which a bibliographic record may be searched and located (AACR2).

agent: The supplier of the serial. The term indicates that the library does not receive the serial directly from the publisher. Instead, a middleman (the agent) handles all aspects of the serial: orders, claims, renewals, and problem solving.

annual: A serial that is issued once per year.

backset: This term refers to the noncurrent issues of a serial. It is used in the context of serial acquisitions.

binder's title: The title that will appear on the spine of the bound serial. Since many serials have long titles, the title may need to be abbreviated. Once an abbreviated title has been established, it should be used for all bound volumes.

cessation: A serial that is no longer being published.

chief source of information: The source of bibliographic data that is to be used as the preferred source from which a bibliographic description (or portion thereof) is prepared (AACR2).

chronological designation: The designation, usually a date, that indicates the chronology.

chronology: The date used by the publisher on the work to identify the individual bibliographic unit of a serial and to show the relationship of the unit to the serial as a whole such as January 1, 1995 or February 1995.

claim: A notice to the supplier of the serial that there is a problem. The notice is submitted on a claim form or electronically. Usually claims are for issues that have not been received. Issues that are defective are also claimed.

class A binding: Binding with full buckram, sewn, rounded, and backed spine. This is the best binding for serials and is generally used for titles that have high use or that the library intends to retain permanently.

collate: To put serials in chronological or numerical order, generally in preparation for binding.

collection policy: A written statement that outlines what the library will acquire.

colophon: A statement at the end of an item giving information about one or more of the following: the title, author(s), publisher, printer, date of publication or printing.

corporate body: An organization or group of persons that is identified by a particular name and that acts, or may act, as an entity. Typical examples of corporate bodies are associations, institutions, business firms, nonprofit enterprises, governments, government agencies, religious bodies, local churches, and conferences (AACR2).

credit: This is a memo issued if the supplier of the serial owes the library money, often as a result of a cancellation or currency fluctuation. This memo must be used against an invoice from the same supplier.

debit memo: See INVOICE.

direct purchase: Directly purchasing a serial means buying from the publisher or a bookstore rather than through an agent.

econobind: Binding in which the original covers are laminated. The spine is glued. It is the cheapest binding possible and should be used for serials that are not to be permanently retained.

econo-plus binding: Binding in which the original covers are scanned and reproduced (basically a photocopy). The spine is glued. It is a relatively inexpensive way of preserving a serial that will have limited use.

electronic journal: A serial that is only available electronically (often through the Internet).

enumeration: The nonchronological scheme used by the publisher on the bibliographic unit of a serial to identify it and show the relationship of the unit to the serial as a whole, e.g., volume, part, issue, heft (the German term for volume/issue).

enumerative designation: The designation that indicates the enumeration such as a volume number.

folio: Any item that, because of its size, cannot be shelved with other material. Newspapers are an example of a serial folio. Usually folios are shelved on special units that can accommodate their dimensions.

holdings list: A list giving the serial holdings (i.e., actual volumes) of a particular library. A holdings list is usually limited to the collection of one specific library. A union list, on the other hand, lists the holdings of more than one library.

international standard serial number: Commonly referred to as ISSN, a unique number assigned to each serial title.

invoice: An invoice is a request for payment. The invoice generally accompanies the material that the library has ordered. Also called a Debit memo or DM.

kardex: Kardex refers to two separate items: (1) the card on which serial holdings and other important information is recorded; (2) the filing cabinet in which these cards are stored. The kardex unit usually has fifteen drawers. Each can hold up to sixty individual kardex cards. A kardex unit can, therefore, hold up to 900 individual kardex cards.

main entry: The complete catalog record for an item presented in the form by which the entity is to be uniformly identified and cited. The main entry may include the tracings of all other headings under which the record is represented in the catalog (AACR2).

masthead: The statement of title, ownership, editors, etc., of a newspaper or periodical. Its location varies, but in the case of newspapers it is commonly found on the editorial page or at the top of page one and, in the case of periodicals, on the contents page.

membership: Membership refers to the manner in which a serial is acquired. For some serials, usually academic or scholarly titles, instead of having a subscription, the library becomes a member of the society that sponsors the serial and is then entitled to receive the serial. A single membership may yield more than one serial or a combination of serials and monographs. Memberships, like other serial sources, need to be noted in the serial check-in system.

monoetching binding: Generally the same type of binding as class A binding, but the spine is glued instead of sewn. It is still a good quality binding, but should not be used for items that are to be permanently retained.

monograph series: A monograph series consists of a number of separate items that are related in that they each bear, in addition to their individual titles, a collective title that applies to the group as a whole (AACR2).

numeric designation: See ENUMERATIVE DESIGNATION.

order number: See PURCHASE ORDER NUMBER.

peer-reviewed serial: A serial in which every article is reviewed by experts in the particular field to determine if the article meets the standards and expectations that have been established for the serial. Generally academic serials are peer reviewed.

periodical: A serial that is published more frequently than once a year.

periodical frequencies:

Daily	Monthly
Weekly	Bimonthly (every two months)
Biweekly (every two weeks)	Quarterly (four times per year)
Semimonthly	Semiannually (twice per year)
(twice per month)	
Irregular (no set pattern	
of publication)	

proceedings: Papers presented at a conference are frequently collected and published as proceedings of the conference.

proforma invoice: This is a request for payment. However, in contrast to the invoice, the proforma invoice requests that the library pay before the material is sent.

purchase order number: A number assigned by the library to each purchase order. It is a unique number that can be used to identify an order.

qualifier: An addition to a title to clearly differentiate it from another serial that has the same title. The qualifier is usually the place of publication.

renewal invoice: The renewal invoice is sent to the library for payment following the return to the supplier of the annotated renewal list.

renewal list: A renewal list, sent by the serial supplier, indicates the titles that are being received by the library that are up for renewal. The list is annotated to indicate cancellations and is returned to the supplier.

routing slip: A slip that indicates to whom an issue of a serial will be circulated.

rub: A rub is a copy of the information found on a serial that has already been bound. By supplying this information to the binder, you ensure that all issues of the serial will be bound in the same way. A rub can be made in two ways: (1) by putting a piece of paper on the spine and rubbing a pencil over it thereby producing a duplication of the information; (2) by providing a photocopy of the spine. Rubs are not needed every time you bind an item. They generally are required only for items for which the binding information has not been permanently stored (especially for items that are not bound frequently).

serial: A publication, in any medium, issued in successive parts and bearing numerical or chronological designations; it is intended to be continued indefinitely (AACR2). The term *serial* is also applied to serial publications that are published once a year or less frequently.

statement: A statement is a summary of all the invoices and credits that you have with a supplier. It is not an invoice and does not require payment.

statement of responsibility: A statement, transcribed from the item being described, that indicates the person(s) responsible for the intellectual or artistic content of the item, the corporate bodies from which the content emanates, or persons or corporate bodies responsible for the performance of the content of the item (AACR2).

supplementary invoice: These generally come only from agents. The agent estimates the cost of renewing a serial since, in many cases, he or she has not been invoiced by the publisher. If the actual cost is higher, a supplementary invoice is issued.

supplements: Additional material that is issued in conjunction with a serial. Unlike advertisements, the supplement is produced by the serial's publisher and generally bears some relationship to the serial. Supplements can be regular or irregular in frequency.

suspension: A serial that is temporarily not being published. In contrast to a cessation, a suspension indicates that the publisher intends to publish the serial again.

uniform title: A title by which a work that has appeared under varying titles is to be identified for cataloguing purposes.

union list: A union list is a complete list of holdings of materials in a certain field, on a particular subject, or of a given type of material such as periodicals or films for a given group of libraries.

Bibliography

Basch, N. Bernard and Judy McQueen (1990). *Buying serials: A how-to-do-it manual for librarians.* New York: Neal-Schuman.

Bourne, Ross (Ed.) (1980). *Serials librarianship.* London: Library Association.

Bullington, Jeffrey S., Beatrice L. Caraway, and Beverley Geer (Eds.) (1999). *Head in the clouds, feet on the ground: Serials vision and common sense; proceedings of the North American Serials Interest Group, Inc., 13th Annual Conference, June 18-21, 1998, University of Colorado, Boulder, Colorado.* Binghamton, NY: The Haworth Information Press.

Campbell, Allan and Irene Dawson (Eds.) (1970). *The library technician at work: Theory and practice; proceedings of the workshop held at Lakehead University, Thunder Bay, Ontario, May 8-9, 1970.* Ottawa: Canadian Library Association.

Chen, Chiou-sen Dora (1995). *Serials management: A practical guide.* Chicago: American Library Association.

Cole, Jim E. and James W. Williams (Eds.) (1992). *Serials cataloging: Modern perspectives and international developments.* Binghamton, NY: The Haworth Press.

Cook, Brian (Ed.) (1992). *The electronic journal: The future of serials-based information.* Binghamton, NY: The Haworth Press.

Edgar, Neal L. (Ed.) (1983). *AACR2 and serials: The American view.* Binghamton, NY: The Haworth Press.

Elrod, J. McRee (2002). *Serial cataloguing cheat sheet.* Special Libraries Cataloging. Available at <www.slc.bc.ca/cheats/serial.htm>, accessed February 14, 2004.

Fiander, P. Michelle, Joseph C. Harmon, and Johnathan David Makepeace (Eds.) (2000). *From Carnegie to Internet2: Forging the serials future; proceedings of the North American Serials Interest Group, Inc., 14th annual conference, June 1-13, 1999, Carnegie Mellon University, Pittsburgh, Pennsylvania.* Binghamton, NY: The Haworth Information Press.

Ganly, John V. and Diane M. Sciattara (Eds.) (1985). *Serials for libraries: An annotated guide to continuations, annuals, yearbooks, almanacs, transactions, proceedings, directories, services,* Second edition. New York: Neal-Schuman Publishers.

Geer, Beverley and Beatrice L. Caraway (Eds.) (1998). *Notes for serials cataloging,* Second edition. Englewood, CO: Libraries Unlimited.

Gellatly, Peter (Ed.) (1986). *Serials librarianship in transition: Issues and development.* Binghamton, NY: The Haworth Press.

Gellatly, Peter (Ed.) (1988). *Libraries and subscription agencies: Interactions and innovations.* Binghamton, NY: The Haworth Press.

Gellatly, Peter (Ed.) (1990). *The good serials department.* Binghamton, NY: The Haworth Press.

Harmon, Joseph C. and P. Michelle Fiander (Eds.) (2001). *Making waves: New serials landscape in a sea of change; proceedings of the North American Serials Interest Group, Inc., 15th annual conference, June 22-25, 2000, University of California, San Diego, San Diego, California.* Binghamton, NY: The Haworth Information Press.

Joint Steering Committee for revision of AACR, a committee of the American Library Association, et al. (2002). *Anglo-American cataloguing rules,* Second edition, 2002 revision. Ottawa: Canadian Library Association.

Jones, Wayne (Ed.) (1995). *Serials Canada: Aspects of serials work in Canadian libraries.* Binghamton, NY: The Haworth Press.

Katz, Bill and Peter Gellatly (1975). *Guide to magazines and serial agents.* New York: R. R. Bowker.

Kinder, Robin and Bill Katz (Eds.) (1990). *Serials and reference work.* Binghamton, NY: The Haworth Press.

Lakhanpal, Sarv Krishna (1986). *A manual for recording serial publications in Kardex,* Fourth edition. Saskatoon: Collection Development, University of Saskatchewan Library.

Langton, Diane Jones and Adeline Mercer Smith (1994). *Free magazines for libraries,* Fourth edition. Jefferson, NC: McFarland.

Lee, Sul H. (Ed.) (1994). *Serials collection development: Choices and strategies.* Ann Arbor, MI: Pierian Press.

Leong, Carol L.H. (1989). *Serials cataloging handbook: An illustrative guide to the use of AACR2 and LC rule interpretations.* Chicago: American Library Association.

Library of Congress, Network Development and MARC Standards Office (2004). *MARC standards.* Available at <www.loc.gov/marc/>, accessed February 14, 2004.

Puccio, Joseph A. (1989). *Serials reference work.* Englewood, CO: Libraries Unlimited.

Serials Department, Northwestern University Library (2002). *Interactive electronic serials cataloging aid.* Available at <staffweb.library.northwestern.edu/serials/iesca>, accessed February 14, 2004.

Serials Section, Acquisitions Committee of the Association for Library Collections & Technical Services (1992). *Guidelines for handling library orders for serials and periodicals,* Revised edition. Chicago: American Library Association.

Smith, Lynn S. (1978). *A practical approach to serials cataloging.* Greenwich, CT: Jai Press.

Szilvassy, Judith (1996). *Basic serials management handbook,* Revised edition. Munchen and New Providence, NJ: K.G. Saur.

Whiffen, Jean (1983). *Union catalogues of serials, guidelines for creation and maintenance, with recommended standards for bibliographic and holdings control.* Binghamton, NY: The Haworth Press.

Index

Page numbers followed by the letter "f" indicate figures.

AACR2. *See Anglo-American Cataloging Rules,* Second Edition
Access points, in catalog record, 79-80
Acquisitions, 15-24
  reasons for, 17-18
Agents, role in purchasing, 31-33
Anglo-American Cataloging Rules, Second Edition (AACR2)
  cataloging, 75-77, 78, 79-91
  check-in, 54, 56, 58
  definition of a serial, 1-2
Automated system holdings
  guidelines for recording, 52-57
  MARC format, 57-64
  punctuation used, 52-53
Automation
  advantages, 127-128
  check-in, 51-64
  disadvantages, 128-129
  impact on serials, 127-129
Awareness of serials, 15-17, 18-24

Bibliography, 141-143
Binding
  covers, 114
  factors in, 111-113
  preparing for, 113-116
  steps, 112-116
  timing, 112-113
Binding slip, 114-116
Brief entries in cataloging, 72-73

Cancellations, 124-126
Cataloging
  access points, 79-80
  alternatives to, 66-74
  brief entries, 72-73
  data elements, 77-78
  decisions concerning, 65-66
  designation, 83-84
  edition statement, 82-83
  electronic serials, 88-90
  elements of a record, 75-77
  International Standard Serial Number, 76, 78, 87
  levels of, 74-76
  main entry, 79, 80-81
  new records, 94-95
  notes, 77, 78, 86-87
  numeric or other designation, 78, 83-84
  physical description, 77, 78, 85
  publication information, 78, 84-85
  standards, 90-91
  statement of responsibility, 78, 81-82, 86-87
  subject analysis, 91-94
  title, issues for selecting, 79-80
  title change, 94-95
Cessations, 7-8
  reasons for, 123-125
  title change, 123-124
Check-in
  access to records, 73-74
  automated, 51-64
  compression of holdings, 53, 55, 57, 58, 61

Check-in *(continued)*
  electronic journals, 64
  elements, 38, 39-41
  gaps, recording of, 53-54, 56
  holdings card, 42-44, 43f, 44f, 45f
  holdings list, 41, 66-67
  information found in, 39-41
  kardex, 44-51, 48f, 49f, 50f
  manual system, 42-51, 43f, 44f, 45f
  MARC format, 57-64
  processing, 97-99
  recording holdings, 43-46, 47-51,
    52-64
  sorting, 37-38
Chronological designation, 2
  in check-in, 53-54, 55-56
  in cataloging, 77, 83-84, 87
Claims
  forms, 107-108, 107f, 108f, 109f
  procedures, 106-109
  reasons for, 105
  when to, 107-109
Collection policy, 17-18
  as reason for cancellation, 124
Cost, 3-4, 14, 17, 26
  as reason for cancellation, 124, 125

Designation, chronological. *See*
  Chronological designation
Designation, numeric. *See* Numeric
  designation, in catalog record
Direct purchase, 29-31

Edition statement, in catalog record,
  82-83
E-journals. *See* Electronic journals,
  cataloging of
Electronic journals, cataloging of, 88-90
Enumeration, changes in, 12-13, 53,
    54-55
Exchanges, 33-34
Extent of unit, 56-57
E-zines. *See* Electronic journals,
  cataloging of

Filing rules
  kardex, 46-47
  shelving, 100-101, 102, 103
Format, 101, 131, 133
  impact of, on serials, 8-10

*Gale Directory of Publications and
  Broadcast Media*, 22-23

Holdings list, 66-67

Indexes, 12
  in binding, 113, 114-115
  recording in MARC format, 64
International Standard Serials Number
    (ISSN), 4
  in catalog record, 78, 87
  in ordering, 18, 25-26
ISSN. *See* International Standard
    Serials Number

Kardex
  components, 44-46
  filing, 46-47
  recording information, 47-50
  samples, 48f, 49f, 50f

Machine-readable cataloging (MARC)
  captions and patterns, 58-62
  holdings, 57-64
  textual holdings, 62-64
MARC. *See* Machine-readable
    cataloging
Monograph series, 3, 13-14

New technology, impact on serials,
    131-133
Notes, in catalog record, 77, 86-87
Numeric designation, in catalog record,
    83-84

Order slips, 30f, 32f
Ordering
 elements of, 25-29
 recommended information to
  include, 25-29
Orders, types of, 29-36
Organization of collection. *See*
 Shelving

Price. *See* Cost
Processing, 97-99
Publication patterns, 6-8
Publishers, change of, 7-8
Punctuation, automated check-in, 52-53
Purchase order, 29-31, 30f, 32f
Purchase through agents, 31-33

Qualifiers, 79-80

Receiving serials, 37-64, 97
Renewals
 direct, 120-121
 terminology, 117-119
 through an agent, 119-120
Retrospective orders, 35-36
Routing list. *See* Routing slip
Routing slip, 98, 98f, 127

Sample copies, 15-16
Serials
 characteristics of, 2-4
 definition, 1-3

Serials *(continued)*
 problems with, 4-14
 types of, 2-3
The Serials Directory, 20-22
Shelving, 132
 guidelines, 99-101, 103
 physical restrictions, 101-102
 policies, 99-102
Sorting, 37-38, 97
Standard Periodical Directory, 22
Standing orders, 34-35
Statement of responsibility, 81-82
Subject analysis, 91-94
Supplements, 9, 10-12
 in catalog record, 85
 MARC format, recording in, 63

Title changes, 5-6
 as a cessation, 123-124

*Ulrich's International Periodicals
 Directory,* 19-20
Uniform title, 79-80
Union list
 elements of, 69-72
 punctuation, 69-71
 purpose of, 68
 samples, 71-72

Verification tools, 18-24

Order a copy of this book with this form or online at:
http://www.haworthpress.com/store/product.asp?sku=5075

INTRODUCTION TO SERIALS WORK FOR LIBRARY TECHNICIANS

_____in hardbound at $39.95 (ISBN: 0-7890-2154-4)

_____in softbound at $24.95 (ISBN: 0-7890-2155-2)

Or order online and use special offer code HEC25 in the shopping cart.

COST OF BOOKS_____	☐ **BILL ME LATER:** (Bill-me option is good on US/Canada/Mexico orders only; not good to jobbers, wholesalers, or subscription agencies.)
POSTAGE & HANDLING_____ *(US: $4.00 for first book & $1.50 for each additional book)* *(Outside US: $5.00 for first book & $2.00 for each additional book)*	☐ Check here if billing address is different from shipping address and attach purchase order and billing address information. Signature_____
SUBTOTAL_____	☐ **PAYMENT ENCLOSED: $**_____
IN CANADA: ADD 7% GST_____	☐ **PLEASE CHARGE TO MY CREDIT CARD.**
STATE TAX_____ *(NY, OH, MN, CA, IL, IN, & SD residents, add appropriate local sales tax)*	☐ Visa ☐ MasterCard ☐ AmEx ☐ Discover ☐ Diner's Club ☐ Eurocard ☐ JCB Account #_____
FINAL TOTAL_____ *(If paying in Canadian funds, convert using the current exchange rate, UNESCO coupons welcome)*	Exp. Date_____ Signature_____

Prices in US dollars and subject to change without notice.

NAME_____

INSTITUTION_____

ADDRESS_____

CITY_____

STATE/ZIP_____

COUNTRY_____ COUNTY (NY residents only)_____

TEL_____ FAX_____

E-MAIL_____

May we use your e-mail address for confirmations and other types of information? ☐ Yes ☐ No
We appreciate receiving your e-mail address and fax number. Haworth would like to e-mail or fax special discount offers to you, as a preferred customer. **We will never share, rent, or exchange your e-mail address or fax number.** We regard such actions as an invasion of your privacy.

Order From Your Local Bookstore or Directly From
The Haworth Press, Inc.
10 Alice Street, Binghamton, New York 13904-1580 • USA
TELEPHONE: 1-800-HAWORTH (1-800-429-6784) / Outside US/Canada: (607) 722-5857
FAX: 1-800-895-0582 / Outside US/Canada: (607) 771-0012
E-mailto: orders@haworthpress.com

For orders outside US and Canada, you may wish to order through your local
sales representative, distributor, or bookseller.
For information, see http://haworthpress.com/distributors

(Discounts are available for individual orders in US and Canada only, not booksellers/distributors.)
PLEASE PHOTOCOPY THIS FORM FOR YOUR PERSONAL USE.
http://www.HaworthPress.com   BOF04